CRYPTS, CAVES and CATACOMBS:

Subterranea of Derbyshire and Nottinghamshire

Graham J. McEwan

Published by Sigma Leisure – an imprint of
Sigma Press, 1 South Oak Lane, Wilmslow, Cheshire SK9 6AR, England.

British Library Cataloguing in Publication Data
A CIP record for this book is available from the British Library.

ISBN: 1-85058-352-8

Typesetting and Design by: Sigma Press, Wilmslow, Cheshire.

Cover design: Martin Mills

Printed by: Manchester Free Press

Preface

Despite the fear associated with the blackness and stillness of underground regions, there is a unique fascination in venturing below ground. Few of us would pass the mouth of a cave without peering in but we would probably have misgivings about venturing too far inside alone and without lights. Over the years, however, many people have conquered their fears and ventured beneath the ground, for practical purposes or simply from the spirit of adventure.

Caves were man's earliest shelters: hiding places, refuges, dwellings where fires could be maintained. Sometimes they were used as burial sites, or places where religious ceremonies and rituals were performed. In these early days caves held more than imaginary terrors, for bears and wolves – even lions and hyaenas – once roamed England and our ancestors may well have had to evict such creatures from caves before taking possession. Perhaps it is a folk memory of such times which makes us wary of deep, dark places.

The story of man's activities beneath the earth is a long one, and this book deals with the rich subterranea of Derbyshire and Nottinghamshire, adjacent counties in England's Midlands. Here we find vast natural caverns; rock-cut hermitages; deep tunnels excavated to mine coal and metallic ore; subterranean sand-mines and breweries and, perhaps the most impressive of all, the tunnels cut for miles out of solid rock to carry railways through the hills of the Peak District.

Many of these underground wonders are accessible to the public and are described in the following pages.

My grateful thanks go to the following for providing assistance and information: Chris Hall; Roy, Barbara and Andrew Quayle; Colin Mather and Mrs Margaret E. Bearfoot.

I should also like to express my gratitude for the assistance given by the staff of many of our public libraries, in particular those of Derbyshire and Nottinghamshire, and the staff of Liverpool Museum and Creswell Crags Visitor Centre.

Graham McEwan

Contents

CAVES AND CAVE DWELLERS

Creswell Crags

Creswell Crags comprise a short ravine to the east of the mining town of Creswell, the north side of the gorge being in Derbyshire and the south in Nottinghamshire. (One can look down the gorge facing west and see the winding gear of Creswell Colliery). The site is famous for the remains of extinct animals and the bones and artifacts of early man, which have been discovered in the caves piercing the sides of the ravine. The most famous of the Creswell caves are Pin Hole Cave, Mother Grundy's Parlour and Robin Hood's Cave in the north cliff and Church Hole Cave in the south. Pin Hole Cave owes its name to a custom that required each visitor to place a pin in a rock pool in the cave and take away the one left by the previous visitor in the belief, it seems, that this would bring good luck. Mother Grundy's Parlour is said to have been the habitation of an old woman reputed to be a witch, while Church Hole Cave is so named because of its narrow tapering entrance. There is no firm evidence, it seems, to link Robin Hood's Cave with the famous outlaw – it is merely one of several East Midland sites named after him.

Human beings have occupied the caves intermittently since about 47,000 years ago, the first arrivals being of the Neanderthal type. About 32,000 years ago, Modern, or Cro-Magnon, Man came to the site, and Creswellian Man made his home here about 15,000 years ago, there being long periods between when they were left to the wild animals. The caves have been occupied in much more recent times including the Iron Age, Roman and medieval periods, but it is for their relics of the Old Stone Age or Palaeolithic Period that they are most well known (see table for time scale). Several excavations have been undertaken over the years at the Creswell Caves, the first being organised in the 1870s by the

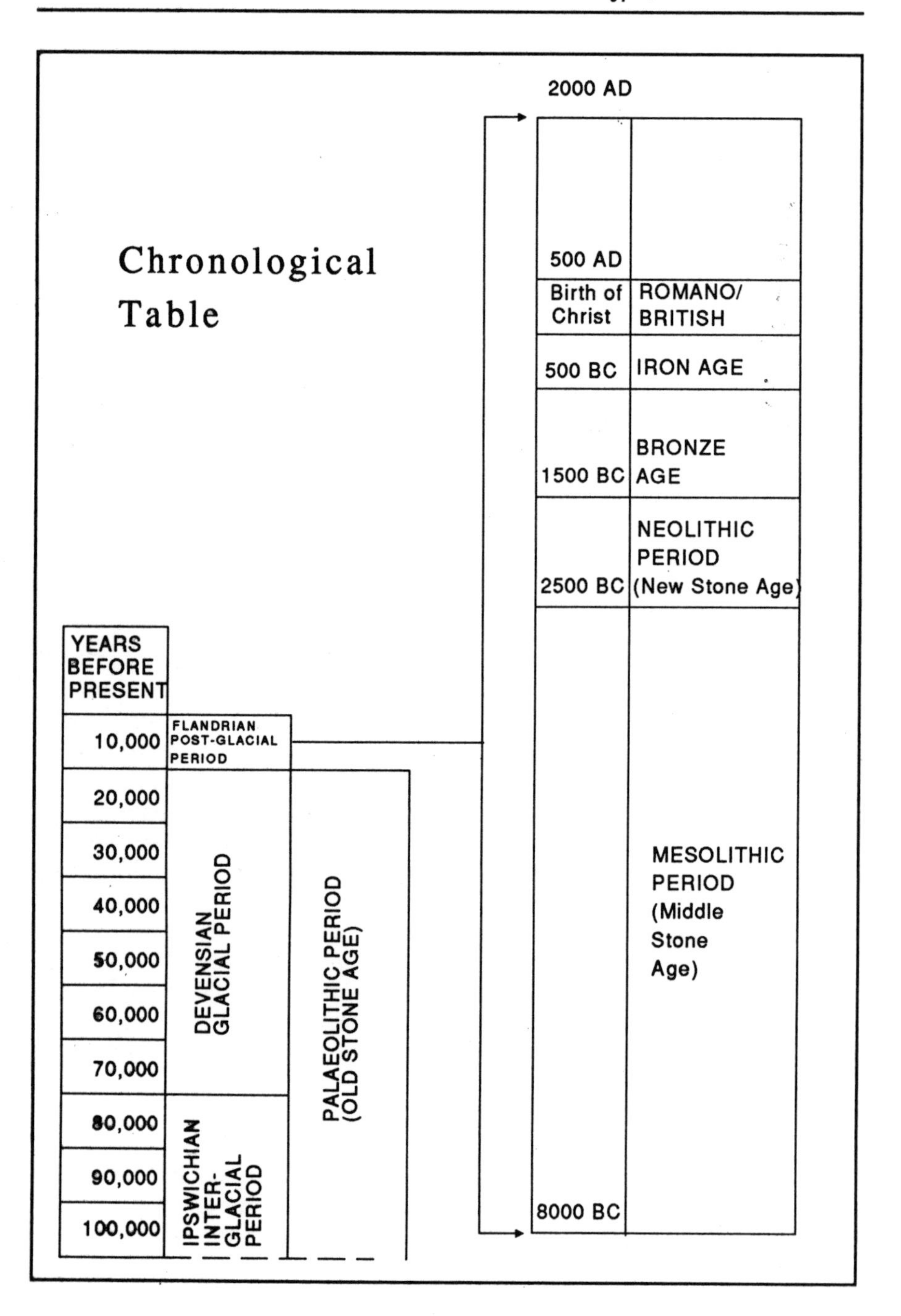
Chronological Table
2000 AD
500 AD
Birth of Christ
ROMANO/ BRITISH
500 BC
IRON AGE
BRONZE AGE
1500 BC
NEOLITHIC PERIOD (New Stone Age)
2500 BC
MESOLITHIC PERIOD (Middle Stone Age)
8000 BC
YEARS BEFORE PRESENT
10,000
FLANDRIAN POST-GLACIAL PERIOD
20,000
30,000
40,000
50,000
60,000
70,000
80,000
90,000
100,000
DEVENSIAN GLACIAL PERIOD
IPSWICHIAN INTER-GLACIAL PERIOD
PALAEOLITHIC PERIOD (OLD STONE AGE)

Reverend J. Magens Mello, a local clergyman, William (later Sir William) Boyd Dawkins, a prominent archaeologist and Thomas Heath, curator of Derby Museum, the group having obtained permission to dig in the caves from their owner, the 5th Duke of Portland. An enormous amount of material – animal bones, human remains and artifacts – was unearthed but the excavation was unsatisfactory in that little attempt was made to correlate the finds with their related deposits and many small, fragmented, specimens were simply tossed aside on spoil heaps. Nineteenth century archaeology was haphazard, with the emphasis more on digging up spectacular finds than on building up a coherent picture of the past. Sadly many finds from this period have been lost over the years and others jumbled together, so that it is not known from which of the Creswell Caves they came.

Pin Hole Cave, Creswell Crags

Further excavations were carried out over the following forty-five years but with one or two exceptions they were even less satisfactory than those of the 1870s. Work was often conducted at great speed, results were not published and finds disappeared into private collections and were subsequently lost.

Creswellian archaeology was put on a more scientific footing in the 1920s with the work of Albert Leslie Armstrong. Although not a professional archaeologist, he was a meticulous investigator and a highly respected figure in the field. Armstrong, born in Harrogate in 1879, was trained as a surveyor and for a while worked for a local firm of architects before joining the Department of Inland Revenue. He had been interested in archaeology since the age of nine and later became a friend of Sir William Boyd Dawkins, by now president of the Committee for the Exploration of Derbyshire Caves. In 1921 Armstrong undertook a general survey of the Creswell Gorge for the Caves Committee and shortly after began excavating in Pin Hole Cave and Mother Grundy's Parlour. He realised the importance of recording exactly where bones and artifacts were discovered in the cave deposits and marked accurately each specimen he found, no matter how small or apparently insignificant. Armstrong carried out excavations in other parts of the country and abroad but it is for his work at Creswell and in particular Pin Hole Cave that he is best known.

Armstrong died suddenly in 1958 since when there have been three further excavations at the Creswell Caves. The first was by Dr C.B.M. McBurney in 1959; the second came ten years later by Oxford University student John Campbell during his research work on the British Upper Palaeolithic Period; the third was in 1974 by Simon Colcutt, a student of Campbell's at Edinburgh University. These were smaller in scale than previous excavations, which had largely cleared the caves of archaeological material, but contributed greatly to our knowledge of life in Palaeolithic times.

The century of excavation at Creswell has resulted in the accumulation of many thousands of specimens comprising animal and human remains and the tools made by the cave people from stone, horn, tooth and bone.

The Creswell cave dwellers shared their environment with a great variety of animals, some known to us today and others which have been extinct for many years. They included: woolly rhinoceros; woolly mammoth; cave bear; hyaena; wolf; wild horse; bison; reindeer; lynx; wolverine and cave lion. The latter was a fearsome beast, considerably larger, it seems, than its modern counterpart. Creatures such as the mammoth and the woolly rhinoceros did not inhabit the caves – parts of

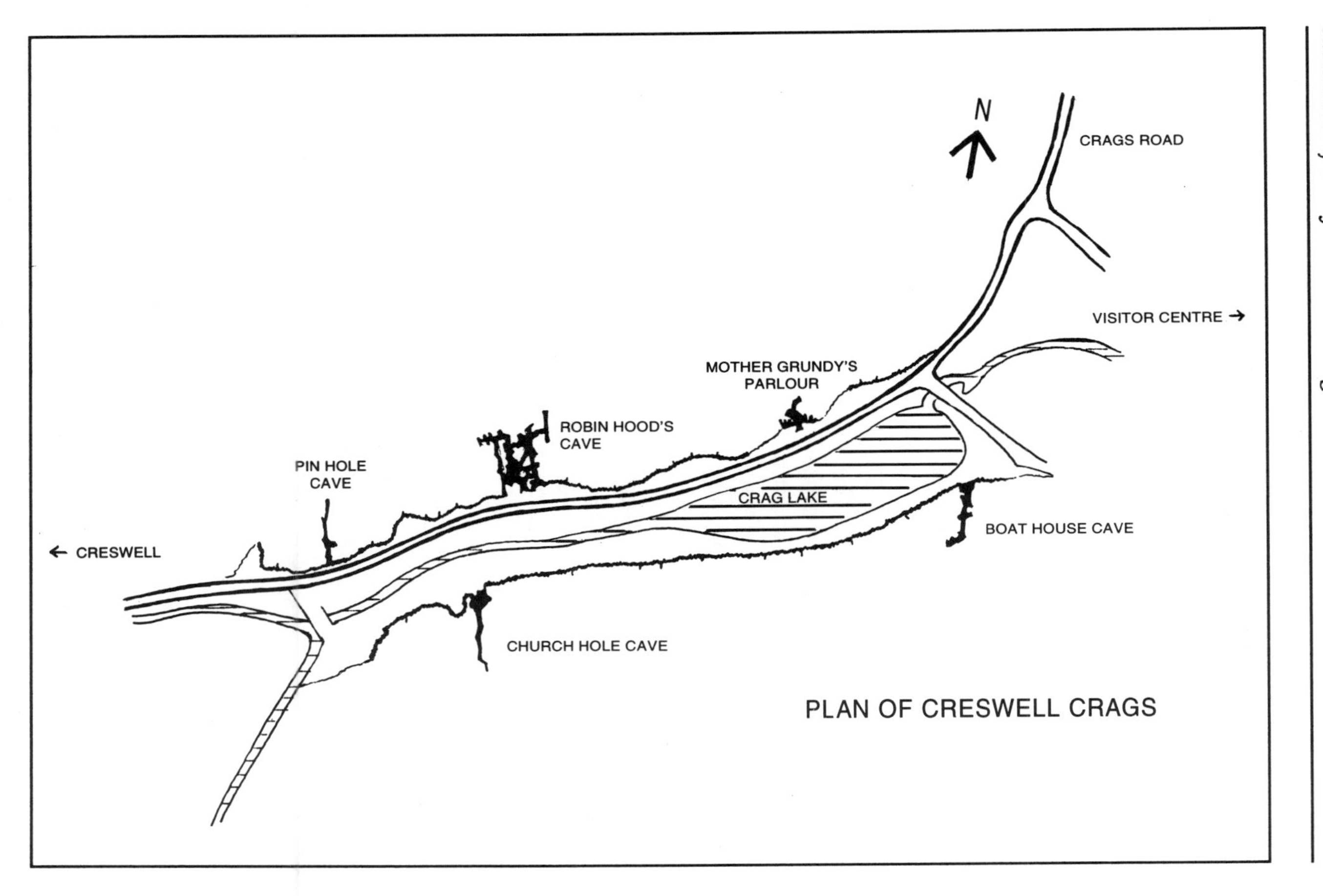
N
CRAGS ROAD
VISITOR CENTRE →
MOTHER GRUNDY'S
PARLOUR
ROBIN HOOD'S
CAVE
PIN HOLE
CAVE
← CRESWELL
CRAG LAKE
BOAT HOUSE CAVE
CHURCH HOLE CAVE
PLAN OF CRESWELL CRAGS

their carcases were dragged inside by the carnivores who killed them. Three of the caves, Robin Hood's, Pin Hole and Church Hole, are known to have been hyaena dens for considerable periods of time. Human cave dwellers also preyed on these creatures, utilising their bones and skins as well as devouring their flesh. These animals flourished in the predominantly very cold conditions of the Devensian Glacial Period, this having been preceded by the warmer Ipswichian Interglacial Period. Remains of the animals from this time found in the Creswell Caves include those of the steppe rhinoceros, giant elk and – perhaps surprisingly - hippopotamus. It is strange to think of these huge beasts wallowing in swamps in the English Midlands.

Pieces of human bone have been recovered from Robin Hood's Cave, Mother Grundy's Parlour and Pin Hole Cave, these all being from Modern and Creswellian Man. The bones are generally very fragmented, the most complete specimens probably being those discovered in Robin Hood's Cave in recent excavations. They comprise part of a jaw bone and a piece of a cranium, these belonging to Creswellian Man and unearthed in 1969; also, an almost complete jaw from Modern or Cro-Magnon Man, discovered in 1975 and now on display at Creswell Crags Visitor Centre.

Although bones of Neanderthal Man have not been recovered from the Creswell Caves, his tools have – consisting of rough axes, scrapers and knifes made from flint and quartzite. Among the many bones discovered at Pin Hole Cave by Leslie Armstrong were pieces which he and archaeologist James W. Kitching believed to have been deliberately shaped into tools by Neanderthal Man. However, later archaeologists are wary of drawing conclusions from these, considering that many of them have been broken and gnawed by carnivores, rather than having been shaped by Man. The tools of Modern Man are more sophisticated than those of his predecessors, which included various types of stone knives, scrapers and boring tools and a range of bone implements. The most impressive artifacts, though, are those of Creswellian Man; of particular note is a bone needle that was found in Church Hole Cave in 1876 – one of the finest discovered in Britain. Also, a needle or awl was unearthed in Pin Hole Cave by Leslie Armstrong and a bone rod, inscribed with a chevron pattern, was found on the same site. Also discovered at Pin Hole Cave by Armstrong was a polished piece of bison rib bearing the inscribed figure of a dancing man wearing an animal head mask, similar to carvings discovered in France and Spain.

The Riddle of Robin Hood's Cave

The two most famous finds at the caves were among the earliest and were the subject of a bitter debate, with accusations of deliberate fraud. The story began on a July day in 1876 when a group of labourers was working inside Robin Hood's Cave under the supervision of Mello and Dawkins. By the light of the candles in the cave Mello saw a small piece of bone which seemed to have something inscribed on it. The bone was carried out into the daylight and then, related Mello, the group saw:

'...the rude picture of the forepart of a horse exactly similar to the Palaeolithic figures that have been found in some of the continental caves. The value of this discovery, the first of its kind made in this country, need hardly be insisted upon.'

Four days later, in the same part of the cave, at about the same level, Boyd Dawkins had the good fortune to see extracted by a workman a canine tooth '. . . of *Machairodus latidens*, an animal whose remains, as all will be aware, have only twice before been found in England.'

The animal in question was an extinct feline of the 'sabre-tooth' variety. When Dawkins saw the tooth revealed in Robin Hood's Cave he is reported to have exclaimed 'Oh My! Pengelly will go wild when he hears of this! It will spread like wildfire over Europe.' (William Pengelly was a former sailor from the Cornish town of Looe who had turned archaeologist and who had discovered a tooth from the extinct big-cat in Kent's Cavern in 1872).

There was immediate controversy over the finds and to understand this we need to look at the archaeological background of the time. Ever since Palaeolithic cave paintings had been discovered at the limestone gorges of the Vézere in the Dordogne region of France, the hunt had been on by British archaeologists for examples of ancient cave art in their own country. Boyd Dawkins was establishing his reputation as one of the foremost archaeologists of the day, his comments regarding Pengelly showing the rivalry which then existed even among fellow British archaeologists. Furthermore, Dawkins had already committed himself in print to the belief that the big-cat had survived from the Ipswichian warm period into the later Devensian Ice Age; the cave find, he said, confirmed this view. However, the discovery of both an example of ancient cave art and a fossil which supported Dawkins's controversial view, all within four days, seemed too much to accept!

View looking down the Creswell Crags ravine towards Creswell Colliery

The suspicion was not so much that the specimens in themselves were fraudulent, but that they had been brought from elsewhere and deliberately planted in the cave. One sceptic was Thomas Heath. While Dawkins asserted that the tooth had been found sealed under a layer of stalagmite, Heath denied this, saying that he had noticed in the earth of the cave a smooth channel, above and below the spot where the tooth was found, this apparently having been made with an iron bar for inserting the object.

It was pointed out by several archaeologists that teeth of the extinct feline could now be purchased on the continent and in the United States and that the bone and tooth were both curiously clean and dry, such ancient specimens being usually damp and dirty. Despite the sceptics, Dawkins and Mello maintained that the finds had occurred exactly as they had described, and the controversy continued, receiving fresh impetus some forty years later with the publication, in 1915, of a book *Ancient Hunters and their Modern Representatives* by the archaeologist W.J. Sollas.

Sollas agreed with the now generally accepted view that the cat tooth was a 'plant' but he considered the horse engraving to be genuine, saying that his information came from someone who had worked on the excavation in the 1870s. Again, Dawkins strenuously denied the allegations of fraud but Sollas's conclusions were later supported by the archaeologist J.W. Jackson who as a young man worked with Boyd Dawkins at the Manchester Museum. He too stated his belief in the authenticity of the horse engraving and the dubious nature of the tooth find, and in the final year of his life, 1979, claimed to know the identity of the person who had planted the tooth, though he would not reveal it. Who could the hoaxer have been? Was it Dawkins himself, hoping it would give a boost to his career, or was it someone trying to discredit him, Heath perhaps? Dawkins had upset him at an early stage by publishing an account of the dig before he, Dawkins, had become involved and in which he neglected to mention Heath at all.

The horse-head engraving unearthed at Robin Hood's Cave in 1876

Curiously the question was re-opened by the archaeologist R.D.S. Jenkinson in his book *Creswell Crags, Late Pleistocene Sites in the East Midlands* (1984), who points out that there is some evidence that the tooth might after all, have been a genuine find: chemical analysis of the tooth as late as 1980 revealed that its nitrogen and fluorine contents differ from those in specimens from other Palaeolithic sites, showing that it could not have come from any of these. However, the levels do agree with other Devensian bone fragments from Robin Hood's Cave – so the puzzle remains.

The horse-head engraving can be seen today at the Visitor Centre at Creswell Crags, along with other artifacts and bones from the caves, which are now closed to the public for reasons of safety and to prevent vandalism. Only the entrances can be seen from the footpaths which run through the gorge – an impressive spectacle with its rugged limestone cliffs overhung with lush green vegetation.

Dream Cave

The remains of ancient animals have been found in many of Derbyshire's caves, a particularly impressive find being that of the bones of a woolly rhinoceros which were discovered in a large subterranean cavity known as the Dream Cave, near the hamlet of Callow, about a mile (1.5km) south-west of Wirksworth, in 1822. The early palaeontologist William Buckland described the find in his book *Reliquiae Diluvianae* (1823):

'On being informed of this discovery, through the kindness of my friend the Rev. D. Stacy, I set off immediately for Derbyshire, for the purpose of examining all its circumstances, and found them to be nearly as follows: In the month of December last, 1822, some miners engaged in pursuing a lead vein had sunk a shaft about 60ft through solid mountain limestone when they suddenly penetrated a large cavern filled entirely to the roof with a confused mass of argillaceous [clay containing] earth and fragments of stone, through which they attempted to continue their shaft perpendicularly downwards to the vein below; in this operation they were interrupted by the earth and fragments beginning to move and fall in upon them continually from the sides, until the roof of a large cavern became apparent, in consequence of the subsidence and removal of the matter with which it had been filled. It was nearly in the centre of this subsiding mass, and at the height of many feet above the actual floor of the cave that the workmen found the bones . . . '

Almost the entire skeleton of the animal, which would have roamed the area during the Devensian Ice Age, was recovered along with some bones from ox, stag and deer and sent to the Geological Museum in Oxford (now part of the Oxford University Museum). Dream Cave, incidentally, is said to have received its name after a lead miner dreamed of a rich vein of the metal at this spot.

The discovery of a woolly rhinoceros skeleton at the Dream Cave – drawing by T. Webster from a sketch by William Buckland

Treak Cliff Sepulchral Cave

On a September day in 1921 several workmen, quarrying surface deposits of fluorspar on the hillside below Treak Cliff near Castleton in Derbyshire, broke into a concealed cave. The cave – which was at an altitude of about 1,050ft (315m) and about 400ft (120m) to the south-west of the point where the footpath to the Blue John Cavern branched off from the main road – was filled with debris. The upper 4ft (1.25m) of this consisted of loose rubble, humus and clay suggesting the debris from a landslide, while under this was a further 11ft (3.3m) of material consisting of huge limestone boulders and chunks of fluorspar. Finally, at the very bottom, was a uniform deposit of fine limestone debris and clay and in this, at a depth of about 12 inches (30 cm), the workmen discovered a collection of human bones.

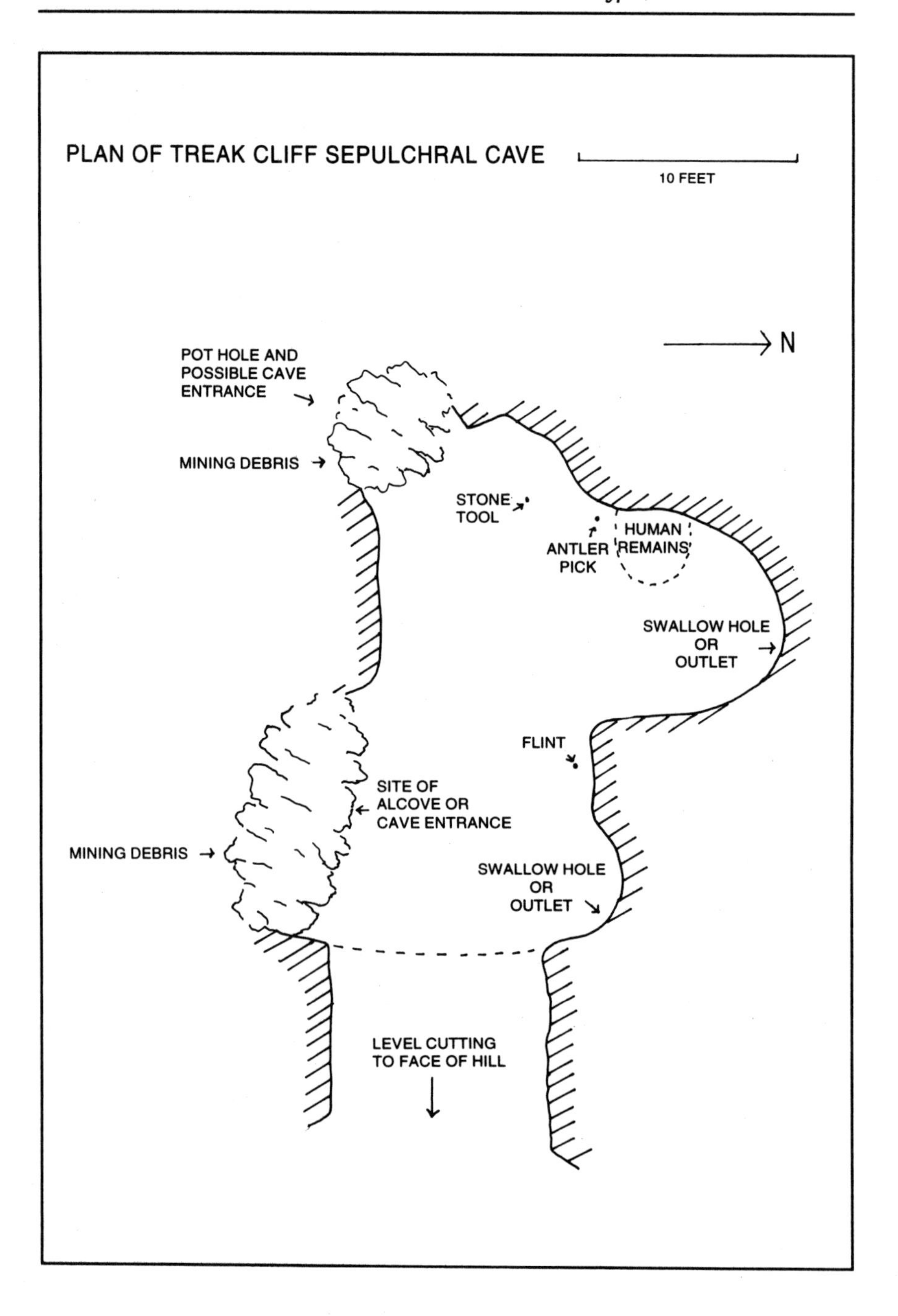
PLAN OF TREAK CLIFF SEPULCHRAL CAVE
10 FEET
N
POT HOLE AND
POSSIBLE CAVE
ENTRANCE
MINING DEBRIS
STONE
TOOL
ANTLER
PICK
HUMAN
REMAINS
SWALLOW HOLE
OR
OUTLET
FLINT
SITE OF
ALCOVE OR
CAVE ENTRANCE
MINING DEBRIS
SWALLOW HOLE
OR
OUTLET
LEVEL CUTTING
TO FACE OF HILL

The men dug the bones out and several, including, apparently, two skulls, were taken away and lost before the find came to the attention of Albert Leslie Armstrong and his colleagues from the Derbyshire Caves Exploration Committee. Armstrong, with Dr. R.V. Favell from Sheffield, began excavations at the cave which was about 20ft (6m) long and 17ft (approx. 5m) across at its widest point. The roof of the cave had apparently collapsed some time after the bones had been deposited and a subsequent landslide had obliterated all traces of its existence. The height of the cave at the walls, at the time of the roof fall, was 4ft 6ins (1.3m). Water had periodically entered from the surface via a pot-hole at the south-west corner (see plan) and had deposited a floor of clay and fine rubble before escaping through two 'swallow holes' or outlets on the north side. It is possible that the pot-hole was used as an entrance by animals and man, though the investigators believed that there was a larger entrance at the south side. This could not be proved, though, due to damage caused by quarrying and the opening here may simply have been an alcove. It was probably only during times of exceptionally high rainfall that the cave was flooded and for most of the time it would have been dry, well-lit and suitable for human habitation, though there was no evidence that it had been occupied regularly.

Although the workmen had taken all the bones out of the cave they were able to give the archaeologists some details of their position, Armstrong reporting:

'The human remains were found close to the west wall of the north alcove, lying within a space of 3ft by 3ft, compacted together with clay . . . The skulls lay nearest the wall, and the relation of the other bones thereto, as described by the finders, suggests that the remains had been buried, not carried there by water.

'This view is supported by the fact that the bones were confined to a limited area, that they were unrolled or unbroken, and that the mandibles were in articulation with the skulls. Though no complete skeleton was found, and a considerable number of bones are missing, the circumstances favour the burial of actual bodies. It is probable that the individuals were buried in the characteristic crouching position, lying east and west, in shallow graves which have been subsequently disturbed by water.'

Except for parts of a thigh bone, only the upper bodies were found -skulls, vertebrae, a shoulder blade, arm bones, a finger bone and some ribs. The lack of the lower parts of the bodies was apparently due to water action. The larger of the two outlets on the north side of the cave was within 7ft (2m approx.) of the buried skeletons, and it seemed probable that, during times of flood, a small whirlpool was created here by the rushing water. This would have scoured away the deposits on the cave floor, the force of the whirlpool being greatest over the place occupied by the leg and hip bones which were carried out of the cave by the flood water.

Besides the human remains, several animal bones and teeth were discovered, including those of dog, pig, sheep, roe-deer, red-deer, rabbit, water vole, fox and ox. Also discovered, about 4ft (approx. 1.25m) to the south of the human bones, and at the same level, was a small stone tool, $2^1/_2$ins (6.25cms) long, $2^1/_8$ins (5.25cms) across its cutting edge and, at its thickest part, $^7/_8$ inch (2.25cms). Of this Armstrong wrote:

'It is probably part of a broken polished axe originally of pointed oval section, which has been re-chipped and partially re-polished at each side, to produce a tapering form with flattened butt, as though for insertion in a socket. The blade is segmented and polished to a fine edge.'

Also discovered, close to the bones, was a primitive and much-worn pick made from a red-deer antler and about 10ft (3m) to the east, a piece of flint was found. It had not been worked, but had obviously been brought to the cave by man, flint not occurring naturally in this locality.

The single complete skull remaining, and several skull fragments, were examined by Dr. Alex Lowe of Aberdeen University who reported that the former, which was in good condition, had come from a boy aged between fifteen and seventeen years. Its shape, short and broad, suggested that it had belonged to an individual of the Bronze Age, he added. Dr. Lowe commented that the remains of the second skull were too fragmentary on which to draw any conclusions. How the boy met his death is not known, but in the harsh conditions of the Bronze Age only the strongest would have survived to maturity. The Treak Cliff bones probably date from about 1,500 years BC.

Some of the bones from Treak Cliff Sepulchral Cave, as it was subsequently named, are now on display at the Cruck Barn Shop in Castleton. They include portions of a skull, but whether these are from the skull of the long-dead teenager, much damaged, or from the second, fragmented, skull I have not been able to discover. The cave itself, which was just above Treak Cliff Cavern, has since been destroyed by quarrying operations.

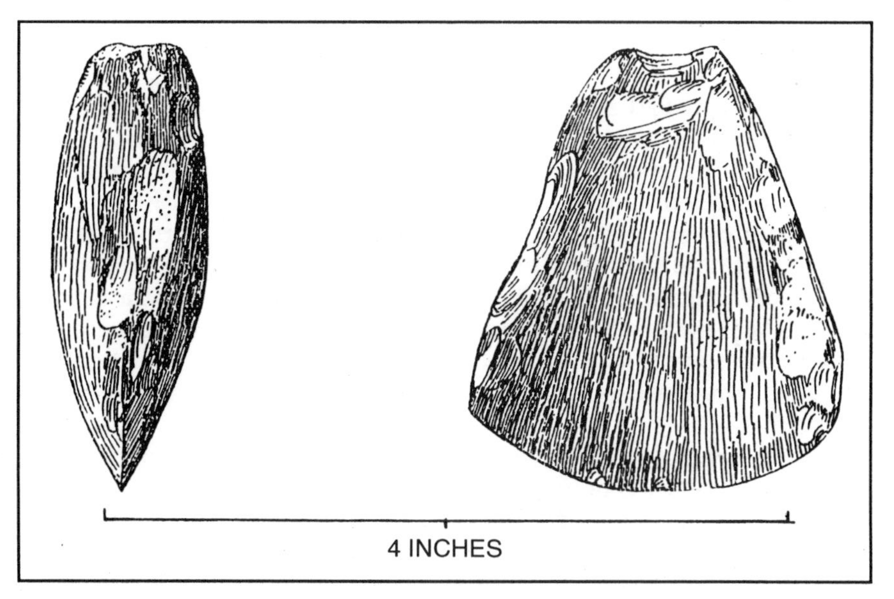

Stone tool discovered in Treak Cliff Sepulchral Cave

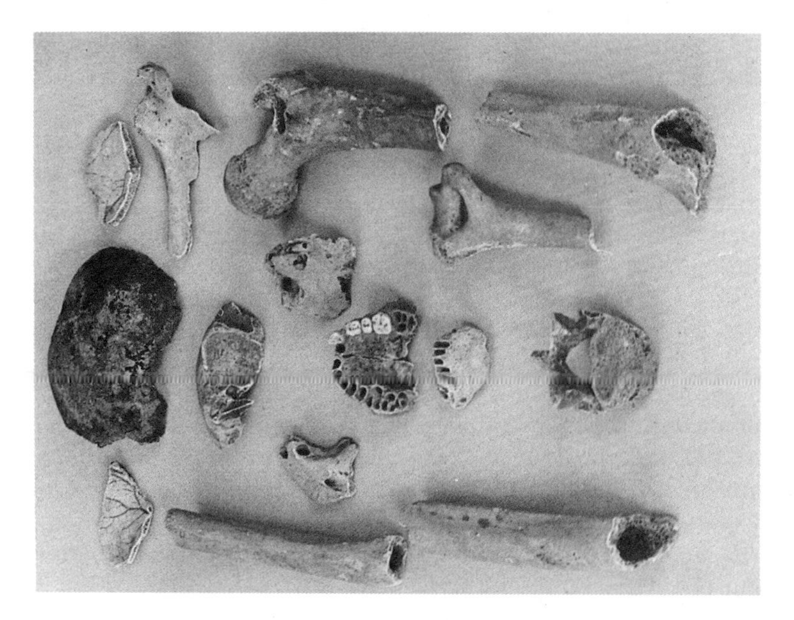

Bones found in Treak Cliff Sepulchral Cave

Dowel Cave

Dowel Cave, situated near the village of Earl Sterndale in Dowel Dale, was excavated in 1958-59 under the supervision of Dr D. Bramwell, being found to contain archaeological material dating from about 9000 BC to modern times.

The main cave is 21ft (6.3m) long with a further very narrow section of about 10ft (3m). Its width on average is about 3ft (approx. 1m) so the actual excavating could only be carried out by one person at a time, a cable haulage system being installed so that buckets of the cave earth could be transported to a group of sorters outside. It was a meticulous excavation, the smallest fragments of bone and other materials being preserved.

The oldest deposits in the cave contained small quantities of charcoal as well as the remains of ancient meals in the form of bones from large mammals, including reindeer, which had been split open. Also found were the tips of several reindeer antlers, these apparently having been used by the cave dwellers for some purpose, and two small flint blades, these being characteristic of the British Upper Palaeolithic or Creswellian Culture. The scant evidence of occupation in this layer suggests that the cave was used occasionally by hunters who were perhaps following the route taken by reindeer migrating through the district.

Evidence of the cave's occupation during the succeeding period, the Mesolithic, was also found, this including split mammal bones, the bones and scales of fish, including those of pike and the skeletal remains of water birds. A lake or marsh had apparently existed nearby.

The most interesting feature of the cave was the collection of human bones dating from Neolithic times, the cave apparently having been used as a family or tribal vault, earlier burials being moved to accommodate later ones. At least ten individuals had been buried here, comprising children, adolescents and adults. All but one of the skulls were detached from the bodies, including a child's skull which was discovered in a sloping fissure in the rear of the cave, a small piece of limestone having been inserted underneath it as if to make it secure in the recess. Despite the bones having been disturbed at different times, it was possible to distinguish two different methods of burial: some of the bodies had been buried in an extended position while others rested in a crouched posture.

Four flints and a bone pin fashioned from the metacarpal bone of a

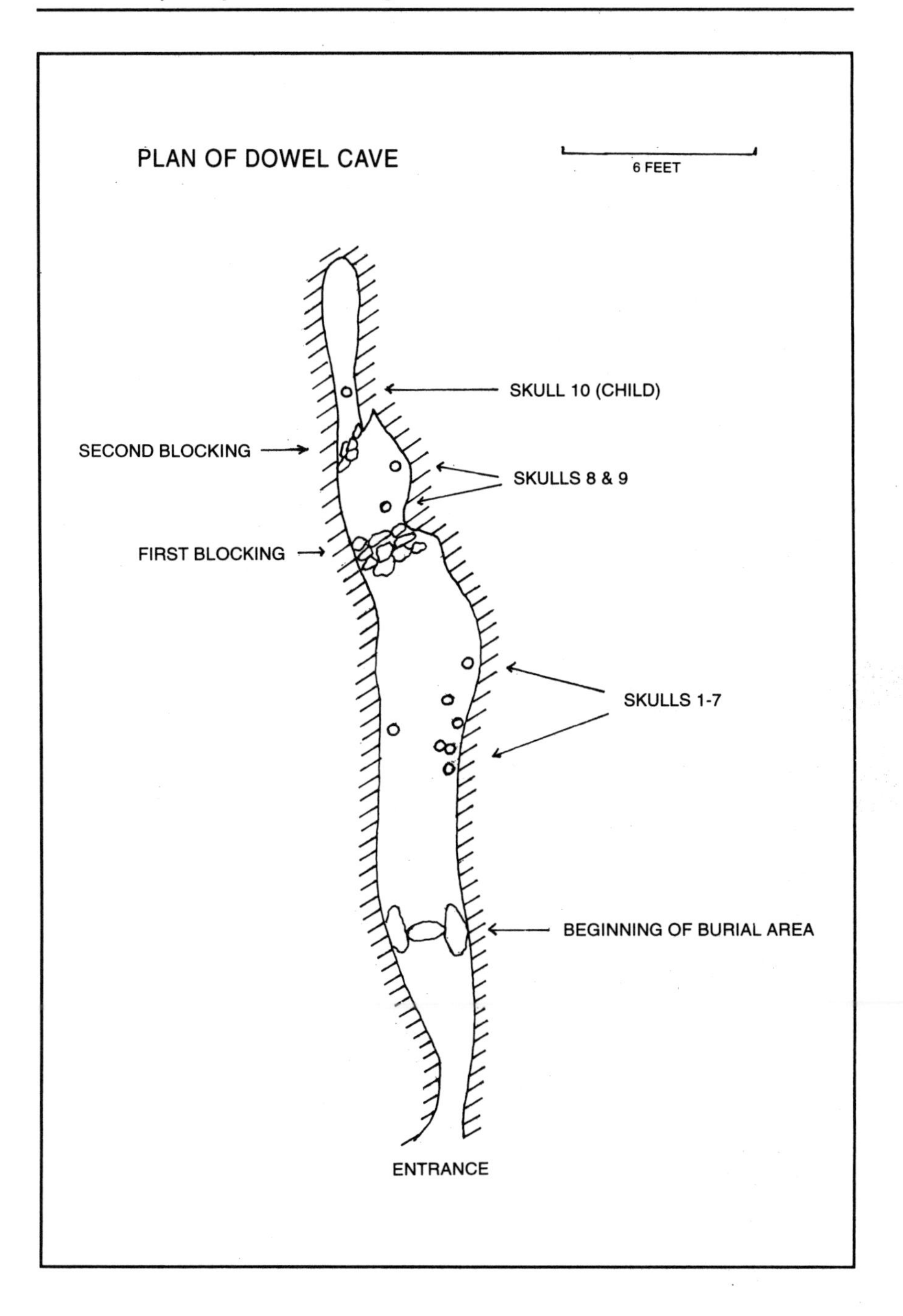
PLAN OF DOWEL CAVE
6 FEET
SKULL 10 (CHILD)
SECOND BLOCKING
SKULLS 8 & 9
FIRST BLOCKING
SKULLS 1-7
BEGINNING OF BURIAL AREA
ENTRANCE

sheep were found with the burials, as were the bones from several other animals including those of ox, dog, deer, pig and goat.

Dating the burial site was not easy, for there was a lack of the usual archaeological material by which the culture of the people who used the cave might be established (the flint tools were rather indeterminate). Certain features of the burials, however, have been found in other tombs known to be of late Neolithic date. These include the practice of using layers of stone to separate burials (known from the Drenthe province of Holland) and the re-interment of detached skulls (recorded at sites in the Meuse Valley, Belgium). A Neolithic date was also indicated by a careful analysis of the animal bones discovered at Dowel Cave, it being possible to correlate these with the known climatic conditions of the Neolithic period.

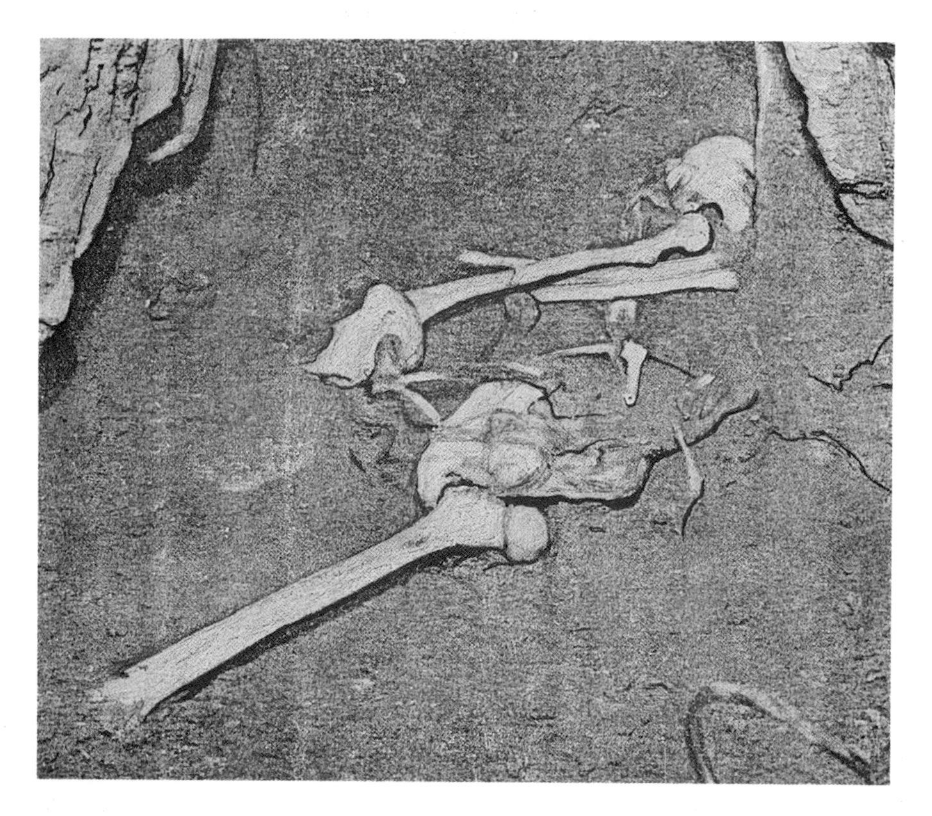

Bones found in Dowel Cave

The bones suggest that the people who buried their dead at Dowel Cave were small with fine features: they apparently herded domestic animals and supplemented their diet by hunting wild beasts, one of which appeared to be a large species of ox.

The layers above the Neolithic crypt contained relics from Iron Age and Romano-British times while the topmost layer, a black mould, yielded old bird-nests, dead leaves, 18th and 19th century pottery and the remains of small animals. There is little to see now at the cave which is situated on the hillside just above Dowel Farm.

Hermits and Anchorites

Throughout history holy men and women have removed themselves from the normal intercourse of everyday life. Some have sought solitude deep in forests, others on lonely islands, while many have withdrawn to the shelter of caves. Their main preoccupation was religious contemplation but while hermits would sometimes mix with the community, to obtain alms for the destitute and perform practical tasks such as repairing roads and cultivating waste land, the anchorites spent their lives totally enclosed, perhaps making garments for the poor, copying books or illuminating manuscripts. They were respected by the community, who often provided them with food. Caves used by these ascetics can be found all over the British Isles, some of them in Derbyshire, but few details are on record of their occupants' solitary lives.

Probably the most impressive of the county's hermitages is the Hermit's Cave at Cratcliffe Rocks near Birchover, 4ml (6.5km) north-west of Matlock. The recluse's faith is evidenced by the figure of the crucified Christ carved in the east wall of the cave. This is in such a position that the hermit could see it from his sleeping ledge in the west wall. The cross is decorated with crockets which seem to represent the foliage of a Tree of Life – at one time, Christianity incorporated symbols from pagan beliefs. A manuscript Rule of Hermits of the 14th century, perhaps contemporary with the sculpture, states:

'Let it suffice thee to have on thine altar an image of the Saviour hanging upon the cross, which represents to thee His passion which thou shalt imitate, inviting thee with outspread arms to himself.'

The cave, which is now protected by railings, can be reached by taking the footpath which leads off the road between Alport and Elton, close to Harthill Moor Farm.

Crypt at St Wystan's church, Repton

The author at Dale Hermitage

Dale Hermitage, in the steep, wooded hillside close to Dale Abbey, is said to have been cut out of the rock in the 12th century by a Derby baker who had a vision of the Virgin Mary. It has a doorway and two other openings and though now consisting of a single large compartment may originally have been divided into two. The cave is overhung by beech trees whose roots seem embedded in the sandstone. The Reverend Sabine Baring-Gould, writing in 1911, asserts that the hermitage was lived in until comparatively recent times and continues: 'When Mr St John Hope was excavating the Abbey ruins, one of his workmen informed him that he had been born and bred in it.' To reach the cave, turn off the A6096 Spondon to Ilkeston road at Dale Abbey into Arbour Hill, then right into the street called The Village. From here walk past the graveyard and Dale Abbey Church and follow the path towards the hillside. Here, there is a flight of steps which leads up to the cave.

Anchor Church

The cave known as the Anchor Church is set in a tree-covered outcrop of rock close to the River Trent, about 2ml (approx. 3km) to the east of

Repton. The cell might have been occupied by an ascetic named Hardulph or Hardulche. The early chronicler John of Tynemouth refers to 'an holy heremyte' called Saint Hardulche who had 'a celle in a clyfte a little from Trent.' John asserts that the saint came from Bredon, this probably being Breedon-on-the-Hill, Leicestershire, where the church is dedicated to St Mary and St Hardulph. This is 7ml (11.25km) south-east of Repton but at one time the parish of Breedon, or the lands of its monastery, might have extended to the Trent. The Anchor Church can be reached by taking the track opposite to the goods vehicle entrance to Foremark Preparatory School on the Milton to Ingleby road, walking across the fields to the rocky outcrop and climbing over a stile in the wooden fence. The cave is something of a disappointment today, much of the rock having been worn away over the years, and the interior walls bearing carved graffiti.

While in the Repton area, mention should be made of the remarkable Anglo-Saxon crypt situated beneath the chancel of St Wystan's Church, Repton. The existence of the crypt had, it seems, been forgotten until 1779 when a workman, digging a grave in the chancel, suddenly fell through into the ancient mausoleum.

The crypt is about 15ft (4.5m) long, the same distance across and 9ft (2.75m) high, a small rectangular recess leading out from each side. Its vaulted ceiling, consisting of nine bays, is supported on round arches which spring from square pilasters set against the walls, the inner ends of the arches resting on four round columns, each of which is decorated with a spiral fillet.

The crypt was originally constructed to house the remains of King Ethelbald who was murdered in 757 AD , a monastery already existing at the site. Subsequently, Kings Ethelbert and Wiglaf were interred here, the latter apparently having made the crypt more ornate during his lifetime in preparation for his own burial – it was probably Wiglaf who ordered the building of the columns, pilasters and vaulted roof. Later, Wiglaf's grandson, Wystan, was buried here following his murder in 849. The Norman historian Florence of Worcester wrote that 'Miracles were not wanting at his martyrdom, for a column of light shot to heaven from the place where he was murdered and remained visible for thirty days.' The crypt became a shrine to the saint, two flights of steps being installed, leading down from the church into the western end of the mausoleum. The steps are worn and uneven, evidence of the passing of many pilgrims, and the walls of the stairway are very rough compared with the smooth stone-work of the crypt walls, showing clearly that they were not part of the original design of the crypt.

In the 11th century King Cnut transferred St Wystan's bones to Evesham Abbey, but the remains of Kings Ethelbald, Ethelbert and Wiglaf almost certainly still rest beneath the stone floor of the crypt.

Harborough Cave

The limestone crags of Harborough Rocks, situated on a hillside about three-quarters of a mile (1188m) to the north-east of Brassington in Derbyshire, are pierced by a cave which has been used intermittently as a dwelling place for several thousand years. The cave is roughly rectangular in shape, being about 25ft (7.5m) long, 20ft (6m) wide and on average 9ft (2.75m) high, with its entrance situated at the south-west corner. In the south-eastern half of the cave the roof is flat but in the remaining part, where large blocks have fallen from the roof, a shallow dome has been formed which connects to the outside by means of a natural chimney.

Two excavations have been undertaken in the cave, the first in 1907, organised by the prominent archaeologist W. Storrs Fox and the second, in 1922, by Albert Leslie Armstrong and his colleagues from the Derbyshire Caves Committee. A great variety of artifacts from several periods was discovered showing how, in succeeding ages, man had made use of the cave as a dwelling place. Details of the most interesting of the finds are given below. The 1907 expedition uncovered two tantalising pieces of evidence which indicated that Man had inhabited the cave during the Palaeolithic Period. (This was the Old Stone Age when human beings shared the British Isles with such exotic beasts as hyaenas, bears and mammoths). The tooth of what was initially thought to have been a hyaena (but which turned out subsequently, it seems, to have been a bear) through which a hole had been bored, was unearthed, also a quartzite hammer-stone. The tooth might have been the possession of a Palaeolithic hunter but, as the excavators realised, it could have been dug out of the Palaeolithic stratum by a later inhabitant of the cave.

The hammer-stone also seemed inconclusive. However, Armstrong's team unearthed further evidence in 1922, including animal bones, some from reindeer, which had been split open to extract the marrow, and two quartzite implements similar to those found in Palaeolithic deposits at Creswell Cave. The larger of these was an oval scraper, 3 inches by 2³/₄ inches (7.5cms x 7cms) and the smaller was a triangular quartzite flake, slightly trimmed. Also discovered were several implements known as marrow-scoops, which were pieces of bone split longitudinally with blackened ends, as if from contact with hot, fatty matter: they are identical to implements found in late Palaeolithic deposits at Mother Grundy's Parlour, Creswell.

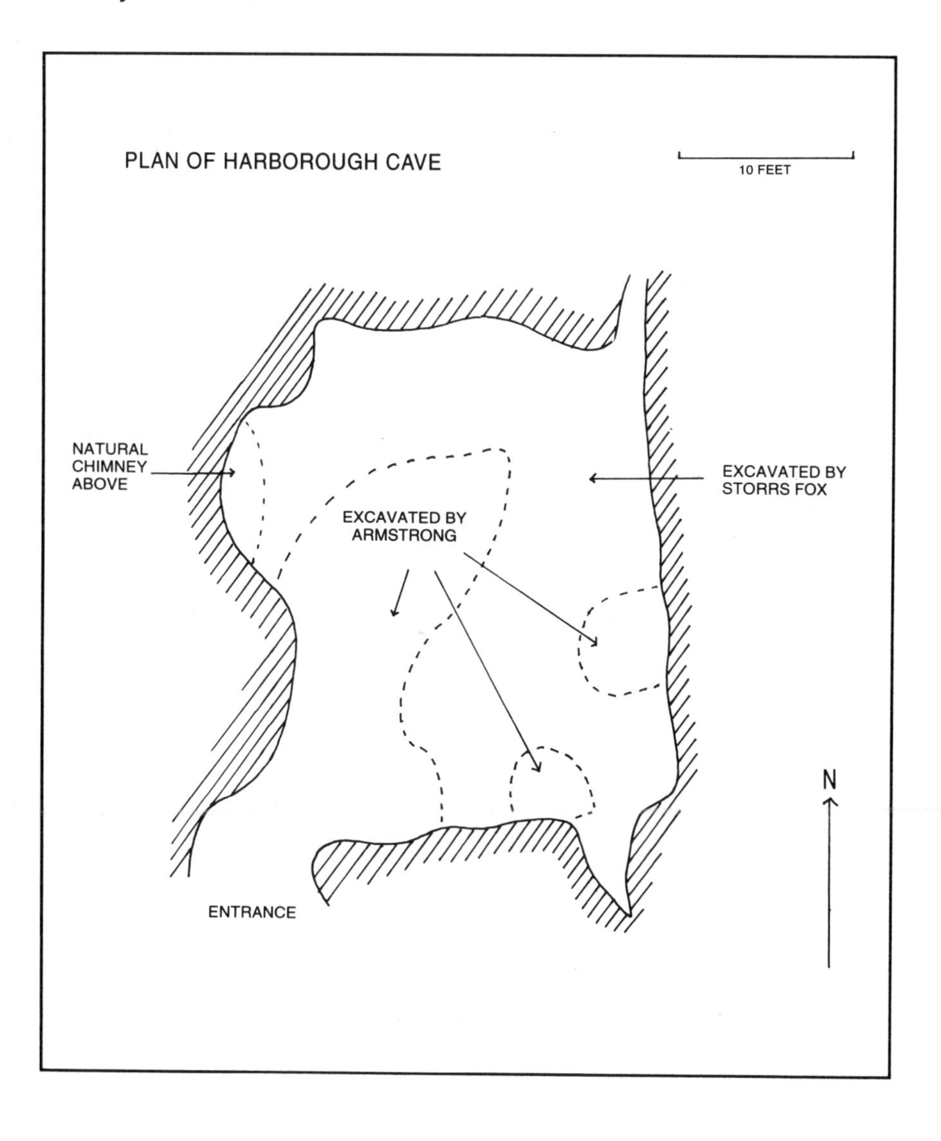

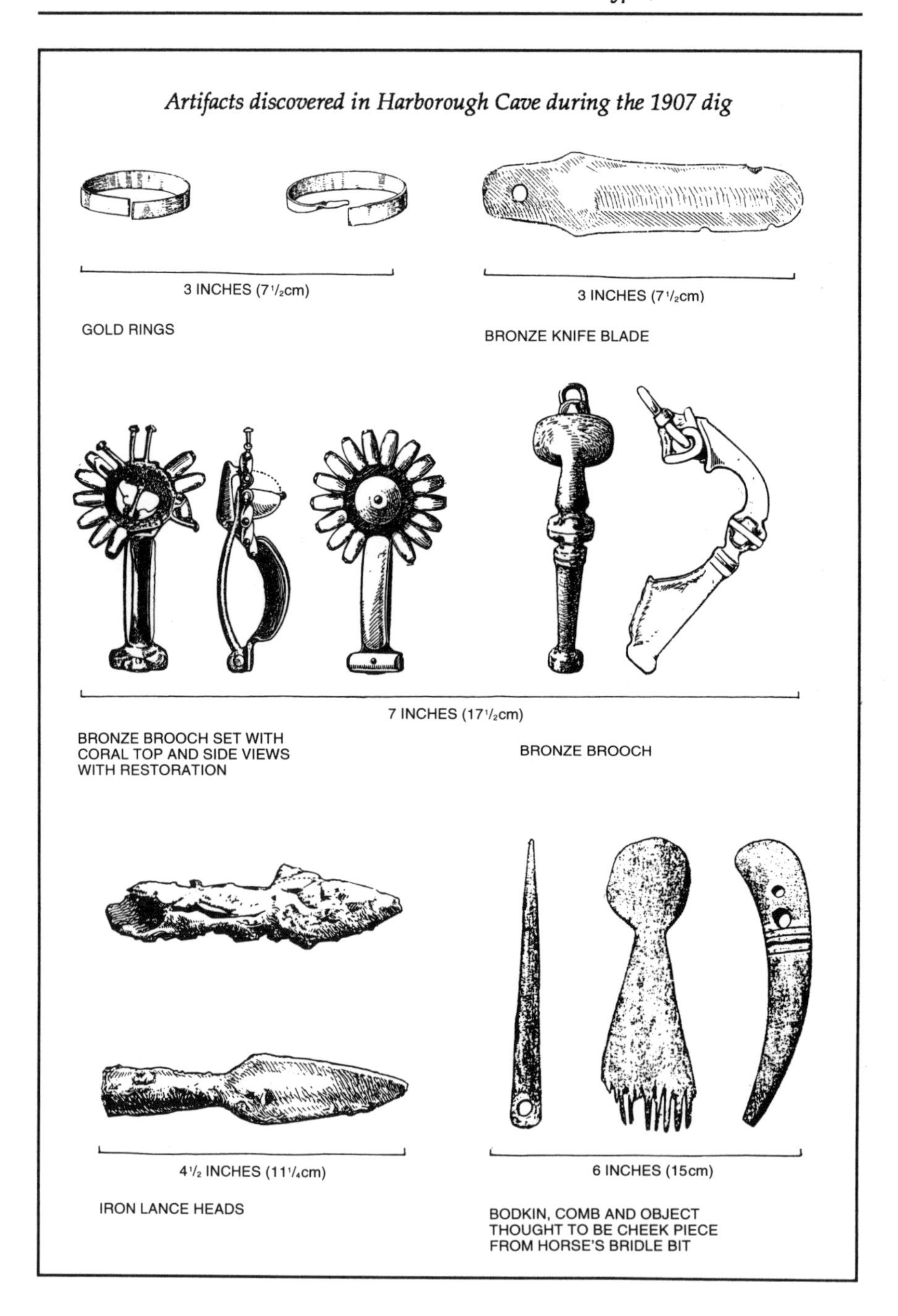
Artifacts discovered in Harborough Cave during the 1907 dig
3 INCHES (7½cm)
GOLD RINGS
3 INCHES (7½cm)
BRONZE KNIFE BLADE
7 INCHES (17½cm)
BRONZE BROOCH SET WITH CORAL TOP AND SIDE VIEWS WITH RESTORATION
BRONZE BROOCH
4½ INCHES (11¼cm)
IRON LANCE HEADS
6 INCHES (15cm)
BODKIN, COMB AND OBJECT THOUGHT TO BE CHEEK PIECE FROM HORSE'S BRIDLE BIT

There was no evidence of Mesolithic occupation of the cave, the succeeding period, the Neolithic, being represented by a few flint flakes, two arrowheads and some pieces of pottery of a type similar to those unearthed at a late Neolithic site at Peterborough.

Artifacts from the Bronze Age included two gold rings, a bronze knife, in a good state of preservation (though its handle, which would have been made of bone, iron or wood, was missing) and a small fragment of reddish pottery which seemed to be part of a cup similar to those found elsewhere in graves of the period.

Artifacts from the Iron Age were more plentiful, and included three finely-crafted bone needles, whorls for spinning thread for weaving and a bone comb which was probably used to press down the weft on a loom (the making of cloth was apparently quite advanced during the Iron Age).

Also found were a bone skewer or bodkin, several tools for boring, and a curious piece made from red-deer antler, which is thought to have been a cheek piece of a horse's bridle-bit. Iron Age pottery was found, as well as a bronze hand-pin of a well-known type, thought to date from about 400 – 300 BC.

Moving onwards in time, there were many finds from Roman and Romano-British times, among which were two coins from Emperor Trajan's reign (98 – 117 AD), lance-heads, knife blades and many pieces of pottery of several different styles.

Perhaps the most impressive artifact to be found in the cave was a bronze brooch mounted with coral and thought to date from the late Iron Age. Four more brooches were discovered of the Roman or Romano-British periods.

Evidence of the cave's occupation during the Middle Ages is indicated by fragments of medieval pottery, and, astonishingly, we find in Daniel Defoe's book *A Tour through the Whole Island of Great Britain* (published in 1724) an account of his chance encounter with a family who, for at least three generations, had lived within the cave. Defoe came across Harborough Cave while looking for a geological curiosity known as the Giant's Tomb (a huge slab of rock on the top of Harborough Rocks). Defoe wrote:

'As we came near the hill, which seemed to be round and a precipice almost on every side, we perceived a little parcel of ground hedged in as if it were a garden . . . we saw no house, but, by a dog running out and barking, we perceived some people were thereabouts, and presently after

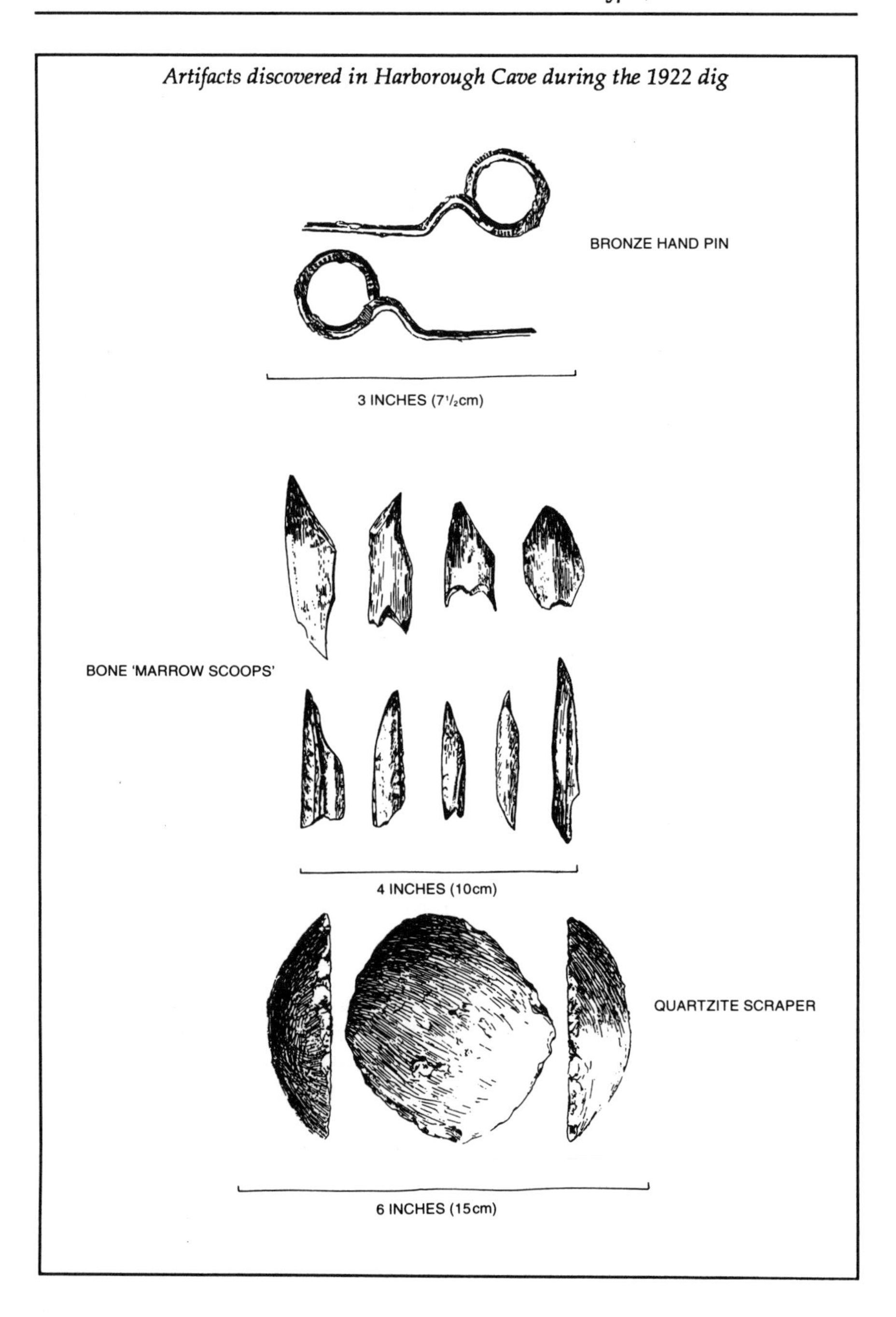
Artifacts discovered in Harborough Cave during the 1922 dig
BRONZE HAND PIN
3 INCHES (7½cm)
BONE 'MARROW SCOOPS'
4 INCHES (10cm)
QUARTZITE SCRAPER
6 INCHES (15cm)

we saw two little children, and then a third ran out to see what was the matter. When we came close up we saw a small opening not a door, but a natural opening into the rock, and the noise we had made brought a woman out with a child in her arms, and another at her foot. N.B. the biggest of these five was a girl about eight or ten years old . . . '

The travellers asked the woman where she and her family lived, and were amazed when she indicated the hole in the rock. Defoe continues:

'"Will you give me leave", says one of our company, as curious as I was, "to come in and see your house, dame?" "If you please, sir," says she, "but tis not a place fit for such as you are to come into," calling him 'your worship' forsooth, but that by-the-by. I mention it to show that the good woman did not want manners though she lived in a den like a wild body."'

On entering the cave Defoe and his companions found it to be much cleaner and more comfortable than they had expected. It was divided into three rooms by curtains, and in one wall was a fire-place (the family had apparently utilised the natural chimney). There were several shelves on which stood utensils of earthenware, pewter and brass; and a whole side of bacon, with a smaller piece, hung by the fire. A sow and piglets were running about by the entrance and a cow was feeding on the grass nearby. Barley was growing in the enclosed patch of ground. The woman told Defoe that her husband had been born in the cave, as had his father before him. Her spouse, whom Defoe later encountered, was a lead-miner who earned, she said, about five pence a day, she herself earning an extra three pence a day, when she had the time, by washing the lead ore. Defoe was surprised at how happy and healthy the family appeared, despite their harsh way of life and primitive living conditions.

The woman said several times how contented she and her family were. Defoe concludes:

'This moving sight so affected us all that, upon a short conference at the door, we made up a little sum of money, and I had the honour to be almoner for the company, and though the sum was not great, being at most something within a crown, as I told it into the poor woman's hand, I could perceive such a surprise in her face, that, had she not given vent to her joy by a sudden flux of tears, I feared she would have fainted away . . . In a word, it was a lecture to us all, and that such, I assure you, as made the whole company very grave all the rest of the day.'

The cave can be reached by the footpath which leads off the road between Wirksworth and Brassington. Harborough Rocks are a spectacular feature of the countryside here, but there is little to see inside Harborough Cave itself which is now used as a cattle shelter.

Harborough Cave

Poole's Cavern

Poole's Cavern, on the outskirts of Buxton, is unusual in that it is not only of archaeological importance, but also a show cave, open to the public for most of the year. Its name derives from an outlaw called Poole who is said to have used the cave as a base for his activities some five hundred years ago.

The cavern was formed by the action over many thousands of years of running water on the limestone rocks. Rainwater is very slightly acidic and, as it percolates through cracks and joints in the limestone, it slowly dissolves it, forming channels. The water carries sand and stones and the scouring action of these assists in the enlarging of the channels. The process was accelerated during the interglacial periods of the Ice Age

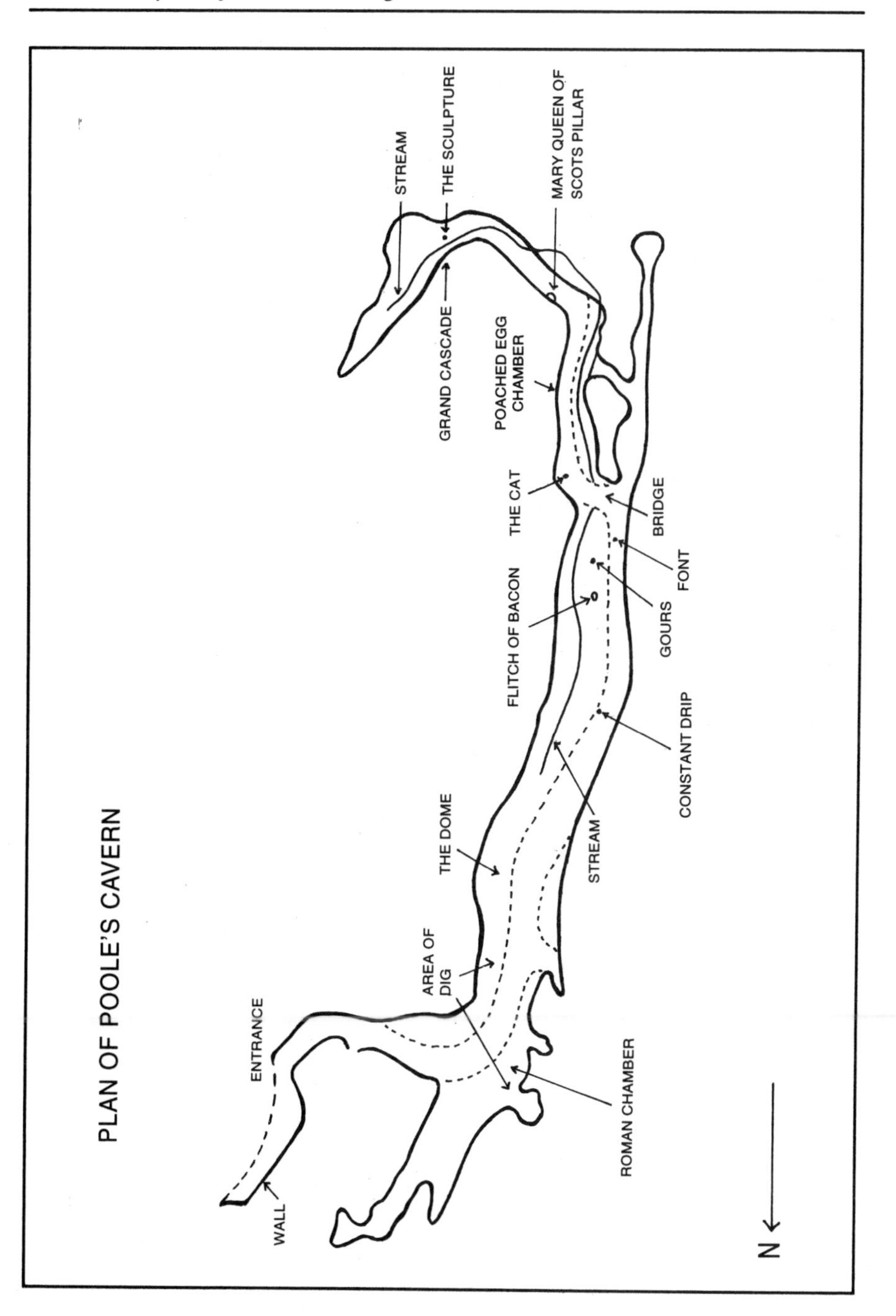
PLAN OF POOLE'S CAVERN
STREAM
THE SCULPTURE
MARY QUEEN OF SCOTS PILLAR
GRAND CASCADE
POACHED EGG CHAMBER
THE CAT
BRIDGE
FONT
FLITCH OF BACON
GOURS
CONSTANT DRIP
STREAM
THE DOME
AREA OF DIG
ENTRANCE
ROMAN CHAMBER
WALL
N

when melting ice formed floods which roared through the cavern. The last great floods occurred some 10,000 years ago with the ending of the Ice Age.

The cave provided a good natural shelter, and it is thought that its first inhabitants were people of the Neolithic period, or New Stone Age (2,500 to 1,500 BC). They probably did not live in it permanently, perhaps occupying nearby settlements and retreating to the cave in bad weather. The interior of the cave is a constant 45 F and the River Wye, running through the cave, would have provided fresh water. The cave was also inhabited intermittently, it seems, through the succeeding Bronze and Iron Ages until eventually the Romans arrived in the area in about 70 AD. Initially, there was conflict between the Romans and the local people, the Brigantes, who may well have used the cave as a store and hiding place. Finally, however, peace was made and most of the bones and artifacts which have been found in the cave belong to the following Romano-British period.

As already pointed out, archaeology, for many years, was far from being an exact science, bones and tools simply being dug out of the ground with little or no attempt being made to correlate them with their surrounding deposits. This was the case with Poole's Cavern, much of the archaeological material having been unearthed by Frank Redfern who in 1854 was entrusted by the 6th Duke of Devonshire with the task of turning the cavern into a show cave. Redfern carried out extensive alterations to the entrance and pathway of the cave during which bones, flints, pottery, coins and other artifacts were uncovered. Some accounts of these were published by the 19th century archaeologists, but they seem to have derived most of their information second-hand from the Redferns and the most basic details of their discoveries are lacking. Some of the finds were exhibited in a museum which used to stand at the entrance to the cave, but over the years the labels of many of the exhibits were lost and finds from other sites were apparently mixed in with them. It is known definitely that Roman coins were found just inside the cave, in the Roman Chamber, Denis Crofton describing these to the Royal Irish Academy in 1867. The coins were from the reign of the emperors Trajan (AD 98 – 117), Verus (161 – 169), Severus (193 – 211), Phillipus (224 – 249) and the two Faustinas (138 – 180). The pottery included pieces of the type known as Samian ware, glazed red earthenware made in France, or Gaul as the Romans called it. One piece bore the name of the potter Paterclinus who lived in Central Gaul sometime between 120 and 260 AD. Jewellery, including several fibulae or brooches, was also found as were iron buckles, rings, pins, beads, tweezers and a bronze stylus.

In October 1981, a properly supervised archaeological dig was begun at the cavern under Dr D. Bramwell, the Roman Chamber being divided into metre wide strips. Over the following two years more than three thousand items were found, most of them being Romano-British. They included human and animal bones, pottery and many beautiful fibulae whose forms included dolphins, sea-horses and chariot wheels. Some of these were unfinished, bearing a flashing as if they had just come out of a mould. Also discovered were a crucible, a mould, globules of bronze and some silver ingots. It is possible that during the Romano-British period a metal worker had his workshop in the cave and made items for soldiers from a nearby fort. It is also possible that the cave was used as a shrine by the Romans who may well have adopted and worshipped Celtic deities. Some of the jewellery found may have been offerings, and the large number of animal bones unearthed may have come from animals which had been sacrificed, cooked and eaten – a large quantity of charcoal being present. Three silver coins of Henry VI's reign were found during the dig, this period supposedly being when the outlaw Poole lived in the cave. Some of the items discovered can be seen in the Visitors' Centre.

Whether the cave was occupied after the Romano-British period is not known, though it seems unlikely that such a shelter would not have been used. The earliest written reference to the cave appears to be in a work called *Sidera* (1580) by Sir Philip Sidney who was guardian to Mary Queen of Scots during her imprisonment at the Old Hall Hotel, which was then the country lodge of Sidney's uncle, the Earl of Shrewsbury:

'Peak hath a cave whose narrow entrance finds
Large rooms within where droppes distill amaise
Till knit with cold though there unknowne
Deck that poore place with Alabaster remains linde.'

It is unlikely that Sidney is referring to Peak Cavern (the only other cave then known in the region) since the entrance to this is vast, and he mentions specifically the 'narrow entrance'. The shadowy figure of Poole might have lived in the cave during the 14th or 15th centuries, the story being well known by the time of Elizabeth I. One early reference to the outlaw is that by the political writer Thomas Hobbes, who was a tutor to the Earl of Devonshire's children (the Dukedom had not then been conferred). In 1636 he published a poem in Latin with the title *De Mirabilibus Pecci* (*Wonders of the Peaks*): part of the English translation runs:

> *'The thing remain'd, but highly worth our view, Poole's Hole, a cave so called, and near us too. Poole was a famous thief, and as we're told Equal to Caccus and perchance as old'*

According to some theories, Poole was not a villain at all, but a political refugee, or a member of an aristocratic family, a legend which has been applied to other outlaws. 17th century diarist Ralph Thoresby recorded in 1681 that the cave was named after '. . . one Pool of Pool's Hall, in Staffordshire, a man of great valour who, being outlawed, resided here for his own security.'

In his great topographical poem on England, *Polyolbion* (1622), Michael Drayton referred to Poole thus:

> *'Of that more generous stock, long honour'd in this shrine,*
> *Of which amongst the rest, are being outlawed here,*
> *For his strong refuge tooke this dark and uncouth place*
> *An heir-loom ever since, to that succeeding race.'*

The fame of the cavern spread rapidly and it received several eminent visitors including, it is thought, Mary Queen of Scots, who, though in the custody of Sir Philip Sidney, was allowed to visit the thermal springs at Buxton to alleviate her rheumatism. It seemed that during one of these excursions she visited Poole's Cavern and asked that the huge stalactite pillar which then marked the extent of the easily accessible part of the cave should henceforth bear her name, which it does. Evidence for the visit is scanty, but the story was widespread by the end of the 16th century. The dramatist Ben Johnson visited the cave, and, in 1633, produced a masque called *The King's Entertainment* at Welbeck, Nottinghamshire, in which he refers to the cave as one of the Wonders of the Peak.

The famous early traveller, Celia Fiennes, came here in the 17th century and gave a lengthy description of the cave of which the following is an extract:

'Another wonder is that of Poole's Hole that's just at the town end, a large cavity underground of great length: just at the Entrance you must creep, but presently you stand upright, its Roofe being very lofty all arched in the rocks and sound with a great Ecchoe . . . I went as far as the Queen of Scotts Pillar . . . '

In the 18th century Dr Samuel Johnson visited the cave and must have found it difficult to squeeze his bulky figure through the narrow entrance and restricted passages. Daniel Defoe (1660 – 1731), another famous visitor, seems to have been unimpressed and struck a sour note describing it as 'another of the wonderless wonders of the Peak'! Sir John Betjeman, however, after his visit to the cave in 1980, wrote to the custodian, Mr David Allsop, who had pushed the poet through the cave in his wheelchair:

'I shall long remember your strength, courage and knowledge in moving my unwieldy body through the vast wonders of Poole's Cavern yesterday. It was a marvellous journey through time, back a million years. It was awe-inspiring and gave me a sense of being one with nature.'

In the early days visitors were conducted through the cave by local cottagers and there were many complaints about their greed. In 1854 the 6th Duke of Devonshire, who owned the cave, decided to appoint a proper guide who would treat visitors with courtesy and also look after the cave, many early tourists having broken off pieces of stalactite as souvenirs. As mentioned earlier, he appointed Frank Redfern, who cut away the floor at the entrance to the cave, so that visitors could walk in upright - previously they had to crawl or crouch for twenty yards before they could stand. He also removed the great bank of earth and stone at the entrance and built a stone wall in the entrance arch partly to stop people collecting water at a spring there and partly to support the road above. He also built a proper path through the cave and installed a series of candelabra on wooden poles. These were replaced in 1859 by gas lamps, which were quite a novelty at the time, and they remained in use until 1965 when the last of the Redfern family, who had leased the cave from the Devonshires for over 150 years, died.

The cave was opened again in 1977, having been purchased by the Civic Association of Buxton who carried out further improvements including the fitting of electric lights.

On approaching the cave today visitors first see the stone wall built by Frank Redfern, behind which may be concealed further relics of prehistoric man. The entrance to the cave is on the left and the path then passes through the Roman Chamber and the site of the archaeological dig which has been preserved as the excavators left it in 1984. (Some of the finds are on display here and others can be seen in the Visitors' Centre outside). The route then passes through a forty-feet (12m) high chamber known as The Dome which was probably hollowed out by swirling flood waters at the end of the Ice Age. Moving further into the cave one sees a stream – the River Wye, whose source is up on the hills above. In the river-bed, there is a circular structure which is a petrifying well, it being fashionable in Victorian times to place objects such as birds' nests and wicker baskets in this to let the water coat them in calcite (crystalline calcium carbonate) the substance of which stalactites and stalagmites are made. Passing on, visitors now see a feature known as the Constant Drip. Here dripping water, over thousands of years, has built up a stalagmite and then, due probably to an increase in the drip rate, hollowed it out to the depth of about an inch. The path now leads up past a gigantic stalactite known as the Flitch of Bacon, which is about 6ft 6ins (2m) long. Sadly, the end of this was broken off by early visitors, perhaps 140 years ago, and a length of about 18ins (0.5m) is missing. (The rate of growth of stalactites has been much debated; it might, on average, be 1,000 years per inch (2.5cm). Other features of the cave here include The Font, the largest stalagmite in the cave, over 6ft 6ins (2m) high and the gours. These latter are terraces of rock containing pools of water and are formed where lime-rich water flows over irregular surfaces. Lime is slowly deposited, eventually forming ridges which dam water behind them, forming pools. The gours here are perhaps the finest in an English show cave. The path now crosses the river and from the bridge here visitors have a superb view, looking down the cave for a distance of about 500ft (152m).

The route now leads through what is perhaps the most spectacular feature of Poole's Cavern, the Poached Egg Chamber, which contains a great variety of cave formations in white, orange and blue-grey. They are said to be unique and have been created by water flowing through the waste from the old quarry tip above the cave. The blue-grey colour is thought to be caused by the presence of manganese, while the orange is from iron compounds. The name of this cave is derived from the tall, slender stalagmites which are surmounted by blobs of the iron compounds, and which resemble poached eggs. Some formations have strange shapes, one resembling an elephant's head and another an enormous cat. (Legend has it that this is Poole's cat waiting for him to return!). On the roof are thousands of straws – slender, hollow stalactites

The Mary Queen of Scots Pillar

– while other formations include the Frozen Waterfall; a calcite Curtain and Organ Pipes. The Poached Egg Chamber has occasionally been used for television broadcasts, such as the performance by the British operatic singer Barbara Segal, complete with candelabra and grand-piano accompaniment.

Visitors now pass the enormous stalactite known as the Mary Queen of Scots Pillar and descend eight steps to reach the end of the show cave. Here the River Wye flows out of the rocks and a remarkable formation known as The Sculpture can be seen. This consists of a group of boulders which, over the years, have been coated with calcite from dripping water and which resemble one of Henry Moore's amorphous creations. Above The Sculpture is a magnificent display of calcite flowstone known as the Grand Cascade, richly coloured with iron oxide and manganese. The cavern is known to continue for a considerable distance beyond this point, the source of the Wye being some 2ml (3.25km) away, but the passage is blocked by boulders which have prevented further exploration.

The Grand Cascade with, below, The Sculpture

Poole's Cavern, situated off Green Lane, Buxton, is well sign-posted and perhaps most easily reached by the A53 or A54 roads which lead into the town from the South-West.

THE CASTLETON SHOW CAVES

Peak Cavern

The approach to this, the most famous of Castleton's show caves, is magnificent – a limestone gorge whose verdant cliffs rise ever higher above the visitor until, at the cave itself, they are some 250ft (75m) high. The actual entrance to the cave, however, is something of a disappointment for it is partially obscured by iron railings and a wood-built ticket office and tea-shop. The cave mouth is the largest in Britain, perhaps the second largest in the world, being 60ft (18m) high and over 100ft (30m) wide. But to gain an impression of how it should look we need to examine old pictures such as those reproduced here. For centuries the cave was widely known as the Devil's Arse, but such vulgarity was too much for the Victorians who gave it the name it bears today. Visitors begin their tour of the cave in the vestibule (see plan) where to the left there is a series of terraces used for centuries by the rope-makers who lived in the entrance to this huge cavern. Traces of their cottages can be seen on the cave walls to the right, and the soot from their chimneys is still visible on the rocks above. There are very few calcite formations in the cave but, in a rift in the cavern roof, there are some enormous white stalactites. At the end of the vestibule the path descends to a gate and leads into a small cave known as the Bell House. From here inwards the temperature remains at a constant 47F all the year round, making it cool in summer and warm in winter.

The route now leads through a passage known as Lumbago Walk where visitors have to crouch, very uncomfortably, for a short distance before reaching a small pool known as the Inner Styx which contains two species of freshwater shrimp. At one time, the only way onwards from this point was to lay flat in a straw-filled boat which a guide pushed under a low arch into the Great Cave. A tunnel, about 16½ft (5m) wide has since been blasted through the rock to by-pass the lake and the marks of shot-holes can be seen in the roof.

View from inside the entrance to Peak Cavern, 1822

The Great Cave is about 90ft (27m) long, 150ft (45m) wide and 60ft (18m) high, this huge cavern having been carved out of the rock by water, over thousands of years. High up on the wall to the right, a fissure once led to a rift in the side of Cave Dale, almost directly above the cavern, but the passage is now blocked. Two passages leave the Great Cave, the lower of these leading through to the cave known as Roger Rain's House, where there is a perpetual cascade of water, fed by drainage from Cave Dale. The second is at a higher-level, leading from the top of the boulder pile in the Great Cave through to a balcony overlooking Roger Rain's House. This is known as the Orchestra Passage, where the village choir sometimes gave recitals for the benefit of visitors.

Visitors now pass into a wide chamber known as Pluto's Dining Room, from where a wide flight of steps leads down to the Devil's Cellar, the River Styx and the Halfway House. This marks the end of the show cave, though suitably equipped cavers can follow the passages for a considerable distance further as they wind beneath the hillside. The passages are flooded in one section by the river, known as Buxton Water, which flows into Peak Cavern's River Styx. The exact origin of the river is not known, but, about a mile to the south, lead miners on Dirtlow Rake diverted water from their workings into the Great Swallow which is thought to be the Peak Cavern drainage system.

Probably the earliest reference to the spot is in the Domesday Book (AD 1086) where Peveril Castle, sited on the cliffs overlooking the gorge, is described as *'Castellum in peches ers'*, this being interpreted as 'Castle on Peak's Rump'. As early as the 12th century the chronicler Henry of Huntingdon was referring to the cave as one of the 'Marvels of England' and it became a regular stop for such intrepid early travellers as Celia Fiennes, who, on visiting the cavern in 1695, was surprised to find:

'Several poor little houses in it built of stone and thatch'd like little styes, one seemed a little bigger in which a gentleman liv'd and his wife . . . One Mr Midleton who was with us said he had dined with them there on carrots and herbs'.

Thomas Hobbes, who visited the cave in 1683, wrote,

'Behind a ruin'd mountain does appear
Swelling into two parts, which turgent are
As when we bend our bodies to the ground,
The buttocks amply sticking out are found.

I'th midst there is a cave: and on hand
A lofty Rock does as supporter stand
Of a vast weight of earth, which else would fall,
So this the midst with safety guards us all,
And now we're come (I blushing must reherse)
As most does stile it to the Devil's Arse,
Peak Arse the Natives.'

In *Moritz's Travels*, published in 1782, the author wrote:

'I perceived to the right, in the hollow of the cavern, a whole subterranean village where the inhabitants, on account of its being Sunday, were resting from their work and with happy and cheerful looks were sitting at the doors of their huts along with their children. We had scarcely passed these small subterranean houses when I perceived a number of large wheels, on which these human moles, the inhabitants of the cavern, make ropes'.

Entrance to Peak Cavern, 1876

James Ferguson, who came to Peak Cavern in 1772 describes how visitors were floated under the arch into the Great Cave:

'Toward the further end from the entrance, the roof comes down with a gradual slope to above 2ft from the surface of a water fourteen yards across the rock, in that place, forming a kind of arch, under which I was pushed by my guide across the water in a long oval tub, as I lay on my back in the straw with a candle in my hand and was for the greater part of the way on the river so near the arched roof that it touched my hat, if I had raised my head but two inches from the straw on which I lay in the tub (called the boat) which I believe was not above a foot in depth'.

W. Bray, another 18th century visitor, referring to Roger Rain's House, observed:

'At this place you are entertained by a company of singers, who have taken another path and ascended to a place called the Chancel, considerably higher than the part you stand on, where, with lights in their hands, they sing various songs. The effect is very striking.'

Such performances seem to have been quite frequent, the Rev. R. Ward in his *Guide to the Peak of Derbyshire* (1827) writing that visitors were 'generally surprised by a concert' and that they experienced mixed feelings of 'fear and pleasure, astonishment and delight'. Probably the most eminent person to be entertained by the subterranean choir was Queen Victoria, who came to the cavern twice, the first occasion being in 1834, prior to her accession. The young princess was floated into the Great Cave on her back and as she arrived in Roger Rain's House there was a burst of song, candles being lit to reveal the Castleton Church Choir, dressed in white, standing on the balcony. The initial effect on the future queen, apparently quite a nervous girl, must have been one of fear and astonishment rather than pleasure and delight! It is said to have been at Victoria's suggestion that a tunnel was cut to make the Great Cave more accessible.

Another well-known visitor to the Peak Cavern was Lord Byron who recorded:

'I had to cross in a boat a stream which flows under a rock so close upon the water as to admit the boat only to be pushed on by the ferry-man, a sort of Charon, who wades at the stern. The companion of my transit was M.A.C. [Mary Anne Chaworth, the daughter of Byron's neighbour at Annesley in Nottinghamshire] with whom I had been long in love and never told it, though she had discovered it without'.

It is not known if early man inhabited the cavern though a tooth from

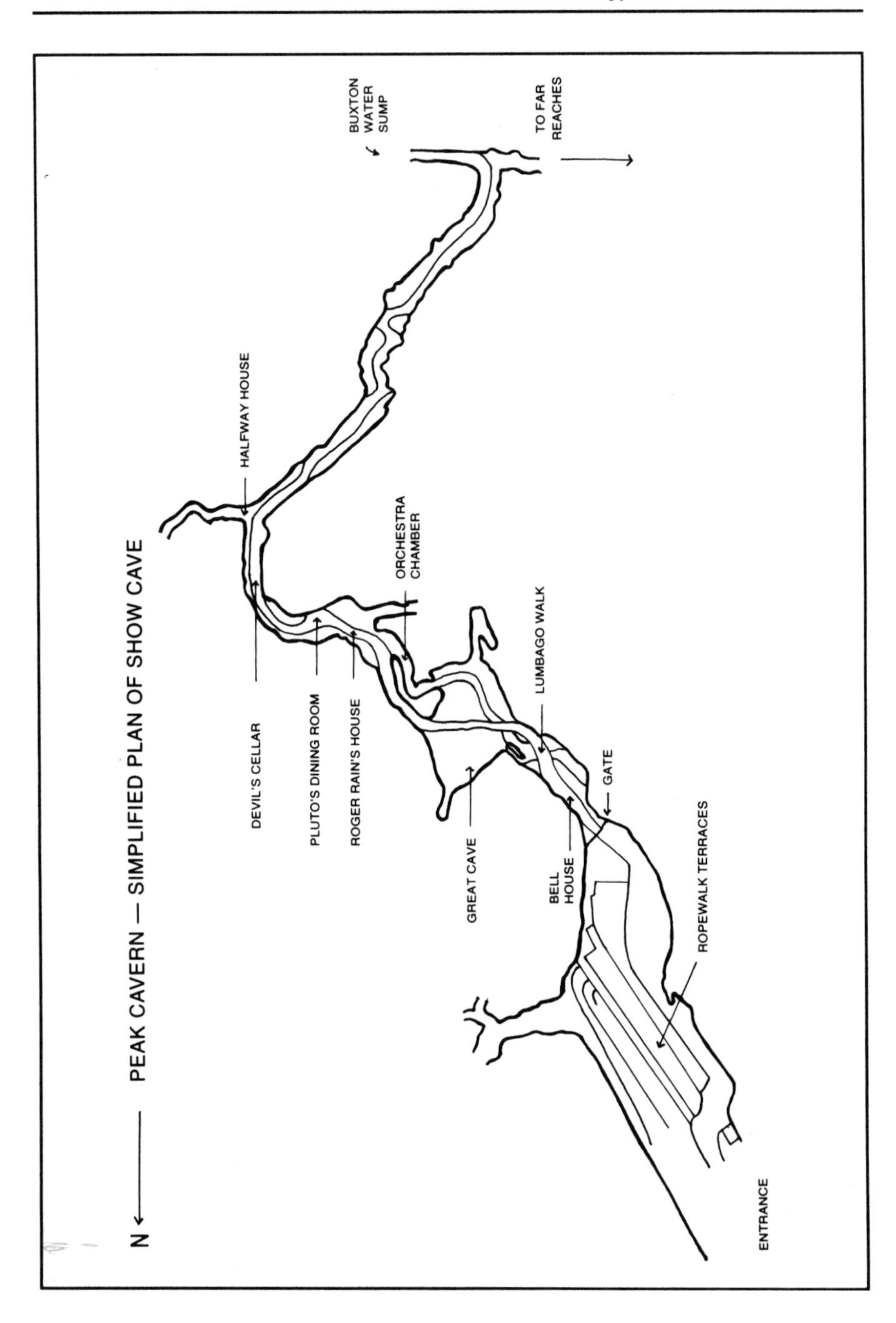
PEAK CAVERN — SIMPLIFIED PLAN OF SHOW CAVE
N
BUXTON WATER SUMP
TO FAR REACHES
HALFWAY HOUSE
ORCHESTRA CHAMBER
DEVIL'S CELLAR
PLUTO'S DINING ROOM
ROGER RAIN'S HOUSE
LUMBAGO WALK
GREAT CAVE
GATE
BELL HOUSE
ROPEWALK TERRACES
ENTRANCE

a woolly rhinoceros, an Ice Age mammal, was found here. The cave would certainly have made an excellent natural shelter from the elements. Outlaws seemed to have inhabited it from early times, the great Ben Johnson describing in a ballad, in 1621, how Cock Laurel, the last 'King of the Beggars', presided over gatherings of ne'er-do-wells in the cave in the late-13th century. The last person to live in the cavern seems to have been one Mary Knight who died in 1845.

It does not seem to be known exactly when rope-making began in the cave, though there are references to the ropes of the fleet which fought the Spanish Armada having been made here and ropes from the cavern were used in lead mining, itself an ancient industry. Rope-making continued in Peak Cavern until 1974 when the last rope-maker, Mr Bert Marrison, retired aged 89. In his youth, he said, there were up to thirty people making rope in the cave, some of them being Dakins and Whittinghams. A census for the year 1846 includes the names Dakin and Whittingham and the families had probably been there for long before that. For many years it was customary for a newly-married couple in Castleton to be presented with a Peak Cavern clothes line and the last time this occurred was apparently in 1969, when Mr and Mrs Brian Woodall were presented with such a gift.

The Speedwell Cavern

In Speedwell Cavern – half a mile (804m) to the west of Castleton at the foot of Winnats Pass – we can look back into history and see the determination and ingenuity of the engineers during the era of the Industrial Revolution. We also gain an insight into the character of the men who laboured for long hours underground in the harshest of conditions, their work illuminated only by candlelight.

Visiting this cavern is a memorable and dramatic experience. Entry is made by a boat journey along a subterranean canal, excavated by lead miners in the 1770s to reach deposits of lead ore deep in the hillside. The original way of entry, used by the lead miners, was a 72ft (22m) deep shaft down which they climbed or were lowered in a large bucket. Today, visitors enter the mine by descending a long flight of stone steps, at the bottom of which is a small landing stage. Here they climb into a boat, which is propelled along the dark narrow canal by an electric motor. (Earlier methods consisted of the guide pushing on the tunnel walls with his hands or an assistant who lay on a board on the boat and

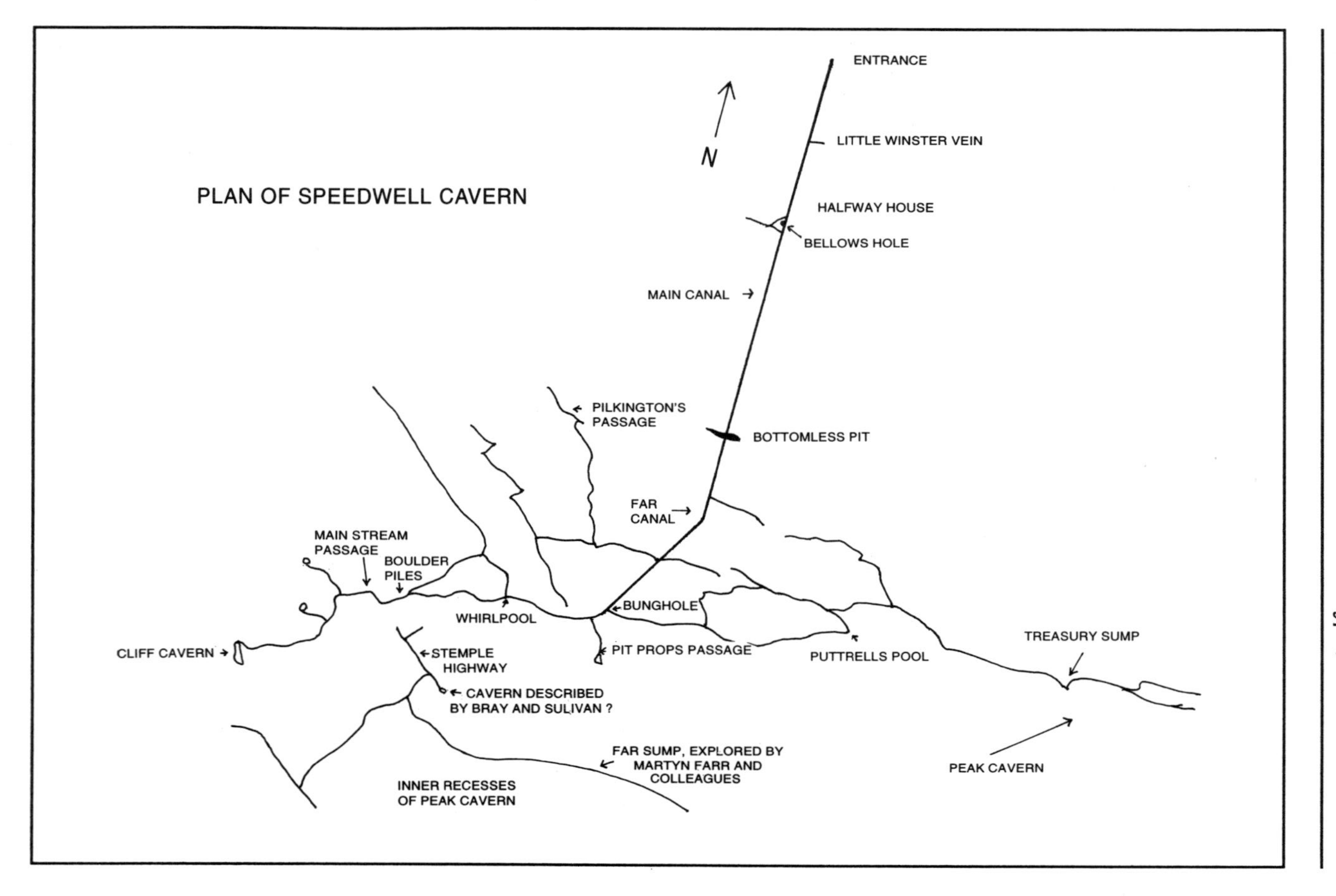

PLAN OF SPEEDWELL CAVERN
N
ENTRANCE
LITTLE WINSTER VEIN
HALFWAY HOUSE
BELLOWS HOLE
MAIN CANAL
PILKINGTON'S PASSAGE
BOTTOMLESS PIT
FAR CANAL
MAIN STREAM PASSAGE
BOULDER PILES
WHIRLPOOL
BUNGHOLE
CLIFF CAVERN
STEMPLE HIGHWAY
PIT PROPS PASSAGE
PUTTRELLS POOL
TREASURY SUMP
CAVERN DESCRIBED BY BRAY AND SULIVAN ?
FAR SUMP, EXPLORED BY MARTYN FARR AND COLLEAGUES
PEAK CAVERN
INNER RECESSES OF PEAK CAVERN

'legged' it along, as did bargees in canal tunnels on the surface).

Several lead veins come into view as the boat progresses, the first of these being the Poor Vein or Little Winster Vein which is less than an inch (2.5cm) wide and which was followed for only 120ft (37m) before being abandoned. Nearby are the Pocket Holes, small openings 12 to 20ins (35 -50cm) wide which were found to contain blocks of lead ore embedded in clay. Next comes the Halfway House, a branch leading off to the south-west for a short distance, used as a passing place for boats and the Longcliffe Vein. This is now walled-up, as the workings are unstable and dangerous, but they probably extend for half a mile (804m) to the west and a quarter of a mile (402m) to the east. Another feature to be seen at this point is the Bellows Hole, a small opening hacked out of the rock where a boy would sit for an eight-hour shift working bellows to ventilate the workings. The marks of drill holes, where gunpowder was inserted to blast away the rock, can be seen in the roof and walls at many points along the tunnel.

It took the miners about seven years to tunnel their way from the entrance to the Bottomless Pit Cavern which marks the end of the visitors' boat trip, and here they step out on to a stone platform. This cavern reaches to about 150ft (45m) above the platform and about 50ft (15m) below it. In the west can be seen the lead vein known as the Faucet or Foreside Rake, which the miners followed upwards by setting wooden beams (stemples) into the rock to form a rough ladder, the remains of which are still visible. The uppermost workings are about 72ft (22m) above the level of the platform.

On the east side of the platform are railings to stop visitors falling into the Bottomless Pit, which contains a lake some 40ft (12m) long by 30ft (9m) wide. Rubble from tunnels and workings was dumped in this lake and legend has it that some 40,000 tons of rock were thrown in and, as this made no difference to the water level, it was assumed that the lake was incredibly deep. However, the geologists J.H. Rieuwerts and T.D. Ford, after examining the evidence, considered that 40,000 was an enormous exaggeration, and suggested that one tenth of this amount would be more accurate. Furthermore, exploration by divers has shown that the lake, far from being 'bottomless' is only about 30ft (9m) deep and that it has natural outlets among the rocks, thus explaining why its level was unaffected by dumping. Initials can be seen cut into the walls of the cavern and, while most of these are probably recent, one inscription almost certainly dates from lead mining days. This is 'C.T. 1806' and was possibly cut by a miner named Charles Tym.

On the south side of the Bottomless Pit is the entrance to the Far Canal, which connects with the Stream Caverns deep inside the hill. Originally the platform on which visitors stand was an aqueduct which connected the main canal to the far canal and which also allowed rubble to be dumped into the Bottomless Pit.

Speedwell Cavern

The Bottomless Pit Cavern is as far as visitors are allowed and the return to the entrance is by boat back down the tunnel, lower and narrower than many photographs suggest, its width being only about 6ft (2m) and its height above water level about 4ft (1.25m). The boat scrapes the sides of the tunnel repeatedly and visitors have to crouch low in the boat. It is uncomfortable for even a short person to sit like this for a quarter of a mile (402m) and the trip is a claustrophobic experience.

What was the purpose of the Speedwell Tunnel? It was not merely an access or exploration tunnel, driven in the general direction of the veins.

If this had been the case there would have been no need to sink a 72ft (22m) deep shaft when the work commenced – a tunnel could simply have been driven inwards from ground level. Nor was the tunnel intended as a drainage sough – its position is such that it could not have lowered the subterranean water levels, and it did not have an outflow direct to the surface. Also, the tunnel was apparently flooded to a depth suitable for boats long before it was completed, any leaks in the rock walls being sealed with clay. Contemporary records are few but the evidence suggests that, from the very outset, the tunnel was excavated with the intention of constructing an underground canal system to float lead ore out of the mine. This was similar to that used in the Duke of Bridgewater's coal mines at Worsley, near Manchester. The engineer, John Gilbert, carried out much of the work at Worsley (though James Brindley usually receives most of the credit) and he had interests in lead mining in Derbyshire, owning shares in two soughs; W. Bray, author of a contemporary book, *Sketch of* a *Tour into Derbyshire and Yorkshire* (1777), describes him as the director of operations at Speedwell. There is also some evidence that the Duke of Bridgewater himself may have been involved in the Speedwell venture, perhaps providing finance.

The hillside contains an extensive system of natural caves and passages, through which the lead veins run, and it seems that at least two ways into the cave from the surface were known before the tunnel was excavated. (The veins had been mined from the surface for some time). One route was described by R Sulivan in *Observations made during a tour through parts of England, Scotland and Wales* (1780). Sulivan wrote that he and his companions descended from the hill above by means of a shaft fitted with stemples – wooden rungs – to a depth of about 420ft (126m). He continues:

'We forced our way with infinite struggles through a narrow space between two rocks, and thence getting on our hands and knees, were for the full distance of a mile obliged to crawl without ever daring to lift up our heads, the passage being too low. Filled with dirt, mud and a multitude of bits of rocks, our progress was painful indeed. On we proceeded till a dreadful noise rumbling along the horrible crevices of the cave gave us to understand we were nearing a river . . . plunging in above our waists, scarce tenable from the impetuosity of the torrent, we carefully picked our steps, and at length arrived after four hours most unspeakable fatigue, at about 300 yards beyond the spot where the subterranean passage [the Speedwell Tunnel] was expected to find an entrance into this dreadful place'.

Sulivan's descent brought him out close to the far reaches of the Stream Caverns, which roughly followed the line of the New Rake Vein. The plan was to intersect these caverns and integrate them into the canal system. The other way in from the surface was described by J. Pilkington in his book *A View of the present state of Derbyshire* (1789), entry being made close to the Bottomless Pit. Both routes are impassable today, though part of Pilkington's route has been climbed from below.

After careful surveying, work on excavating the tunnel began in the spring or summer of 1771. At this stage it was known as the Oakden Level, the work being carried out by Ralph Oakden & Partners of Stafford. The tunnel may have acquired its present name from a public house, thought to have been called the Speedwell Tavern, which is now the shop standing outside the cavern. Following the sinking of the shaft, the work of tunnelling inward began. Holes were drilled in the rock, each being $1^1/_8$ins (approx. 3cm) in diameter and 15ins (37cms) deep. Each hole would have taken about two hours to drill, one man holding the drill and turning it while another hammered it in. Two pairs of men would have worked side by side. When about twenty holes had been drilled, they were filled with gunpowder and packed with clay plugs through which fuses were inserted. When the fuses were lit, the men quickly retired to a safe distance. Still visible in the tunnel is an alcove dug into the wall which was used as a refuge while blasting was in progress – it would obviously have been a tight squeeze for four men! When the gunpowder exploded a great blast of smoke dust and debris would have come down the tunnel.

The rubble was loaded on to barges and floated down the flooded tunnel back to the entrance, where it was lifted to the surface. The boats were shaped like punts and were about 12ft (approx. 4m) long and 3ft (1m) wide. They were propelled by boatmen pulling on pegs set into the tunnel walls. As the men could not have worked thigh-deep in water, clay dams were possibly constructed, which would have been demolished as the tunnel progressed. The tunnel would probably have advanced at a rate of about 4ft 6ins (1.3m) per week, the miners reaching the Bottomless Pit Cavern late in 1778 or early the following year. The Far Canal, which connected the level with the innermost Stream Caverns, was apparently completed in 1783.

Something of a mystery concerns the steps at the entrance to the cavern. As already mentioned, the original means of entry to the mine consisted of a deep shaft but a long flight of stone steps was built shortly after. The mine owners would hardly have gone to the expense of installing these for the benefit of the miners or early tourists; Rieuwerts and Ford have suggested that the steps were intended to be used as an inclined plane, to draw ore-containing boats to the surface, the power for this being provided by a horse-gin. The steps seen today are recent but the arched stone roof above them is original and over 200 years old.

The Far Canal and Stream Caverns

The Far Canal continues beyond the Bottomless Pit, turning in a south-westerly direction. In this length of the passage, lies the partially submerged wreck of an old lead miners' boat. Further on, the tunnel divides at a point known as the Bung Hole where there is an 18ft (5.5m) high stone dam containing a huge, tapered wooden bung. The dam was built across the entrance to the lower part of the passage to keep water at a uniform depth in the upper part (see plan). The bung could be removed to lower the water level in the upper stream if necessary. Several sets of initials, dating from the late-18th century, are carved into the rock walls near the dam: J.T., J.N. and J.I.B. are thought to have been the miners John Tym, John Nall and John Bradbury. The downstream branch, the Bung Hole Passage, leads off to the east while the canal continues in a westerly direction. At a point about 80ft (24m) from the Bung Hole a short canal branches off to the south. This is known as Pit Props Passage due to the timbers set across its entrance to support a wooden dam that was built by Arthur Ollerenshaw in the 1920s to maintain the level of water in the canal during a drought. The passage leads into extensive mine workings.

The man-made canal terminates near the Whirlpool, but the natural waterway continues in a westerly direction, being known as the Main Stream Passage. Here, the miners installed a wooden floor supported on beams set into the rock walls, the stream flowing on underneath. Lead ore was carried along this on sledges, or in wheeled containers back to the Whirlpool, where it was loaded onto boats to be floated back out down the canal. In the tunnel roof above the wooden floor, at a point known as the Boulder Piles, are several blocked holes and these are thought to have once communicated with a passage known as Stemple Highway, which is described in more detail later. The initials M.R. and

B.T. found near the Boulder Piles were probably carved by Mark Royse and Benjamin Tym.

Several natural passages branch off to the north-west of the Far Canal and Main Stream Passage and these also contain evidence of the miners' activities. One of these, Pilkington's Passage, is thought to be part of the route by which J Pilkington entered the caverns as mentioned earlier and it leads to several vertical rifts or avens fitted with stemples. The remains of a corve and pulling harness and a riddle have been found here. The Main Stream Passage itself continues in a westerly direction for about a quarter of a mile (402m) before reaching a 10ft (3m) high waterfall. This marks the entrance to a further short passage which ends in Cliff Cavern. Near to the waterfall, scratched on the wall, is a picture of a bottle being poured into a glass and the inscription:

'A Health to all Mines and Mentainers of Mines.
J.I.B., M.N. Oct.20th 1781'

These initials could be those of John Bradbury (mentioned previously) and Matthew Nall, and the inscription was probably carved when the Far Canal finally broke through into the Stream Caverns.

The eastern branch of the Stream Caverns terminates at Treasury Sump, where the water disappears underground. The first section, Near Bung Hole Passage, ends at Puttrell's Pool, this marking the limit of the lead miners' activities. The ore seems to have been mined in caverns above the passageway and then tipped through two holes. These are now blocked with boulders, but one contains the remains of a chute. Just to the east of this, the miners built a dressing floor over a culvert and here the ore was washed. A wooden plankway, like that near the Boulder Piles, extended from here upstream towards the dam, over which the ore was lifted to be loaded into boats and transported out of the mine. Sockets can be seen in the rock walls above the dam, marking the site of the wooden lifting apparatus or stow.

The Stream Caverns of the Speedwell System are, in places, very close to the inner passages of Peak Cavern, but until recently there was no evidence of a 'dry' connection. However, in 1982, cave diver Martyn Farr made a remarkable discovery. With his companions, Farr had travelled through Peak Cavern to the Far Sump, the western limit, above water level, of the cave. Here, with diving equipment, he entered the water-filled underground passageway, swimming along for about 480yds (432m) before being able to surface. The passage now continued above water level and Farr explored it for about 328yds (295m) as it twisted and turned, eventually coming to a 'T' junction. Farr, in his book, *The Great Caving Adventure* (1984), continues:

'Thoughts of the exit suddenly assumed a priority and of an instant it seemed a good idea to build a small cairn. There was a prominent boulder at this point and before I could place a rock on top of it something odd became apparent, scratch marks? A closer inspection indeed revealed the splintered marks inflicted by a small pick hammer, unquestionable proof that I was not the first to tread this route . . . some long forgotten, probably unrecorded, miner had been here before.'

Farr made several attempts to discover the route by which the Speedwell miners had reached this point but without success. He did find much evidence of their activities, though, including a long stemple-filled aven, this subsequently being called Stemple Highway. The position of this passage suggests that it was once connected by a route now lost, to the Boulder Piles section of the Speedwell Stream Caverns.

Treak Cliff and Blue John Caverns

Treak Cliff hill is situated on the north side of Winnats Pass, being about 490ft (147m) high and $^{5}/_{8}$th of a mile (1km) long. Within the hill are two well-known caves, Treak Cliff Cavern and Blue John Cavern, in which is the famous Blue John Mine.

Blue John is a valuable ornamental variety of fluorspar (calcium fluoride). It differs from other fluorspars in that it has distinctive bands of colour running through it, most characteristically purplish blue. Deposits of fluorspar similar to Blue John are known in other parts of the world, but the banded patterns of Blue John are unique to Treak Cliff and a few other localities in the Castleton area. The exact cause of the colouration of the Blue John stone is still unclear and there have been many theories, the latest of which suggests the displacement, thousands of years ago, of some calcium atoms from their normal position within the colourless fluorspar crystals. The displaced atoms form groups which collect in defects in the mineral and absorb and scatter light, creating the blue colouration.

Both caverns were formed by the action of water. The rocks of Treak Cliff, Winnats Pass and the surrounding area are of limestone formed during the Carboniferous Period which ended about 210 million years ago. The rock was once the sediment of an ancient sea bed, shown by the fossils of sea creatures seen in the caves. Over millions of years, the

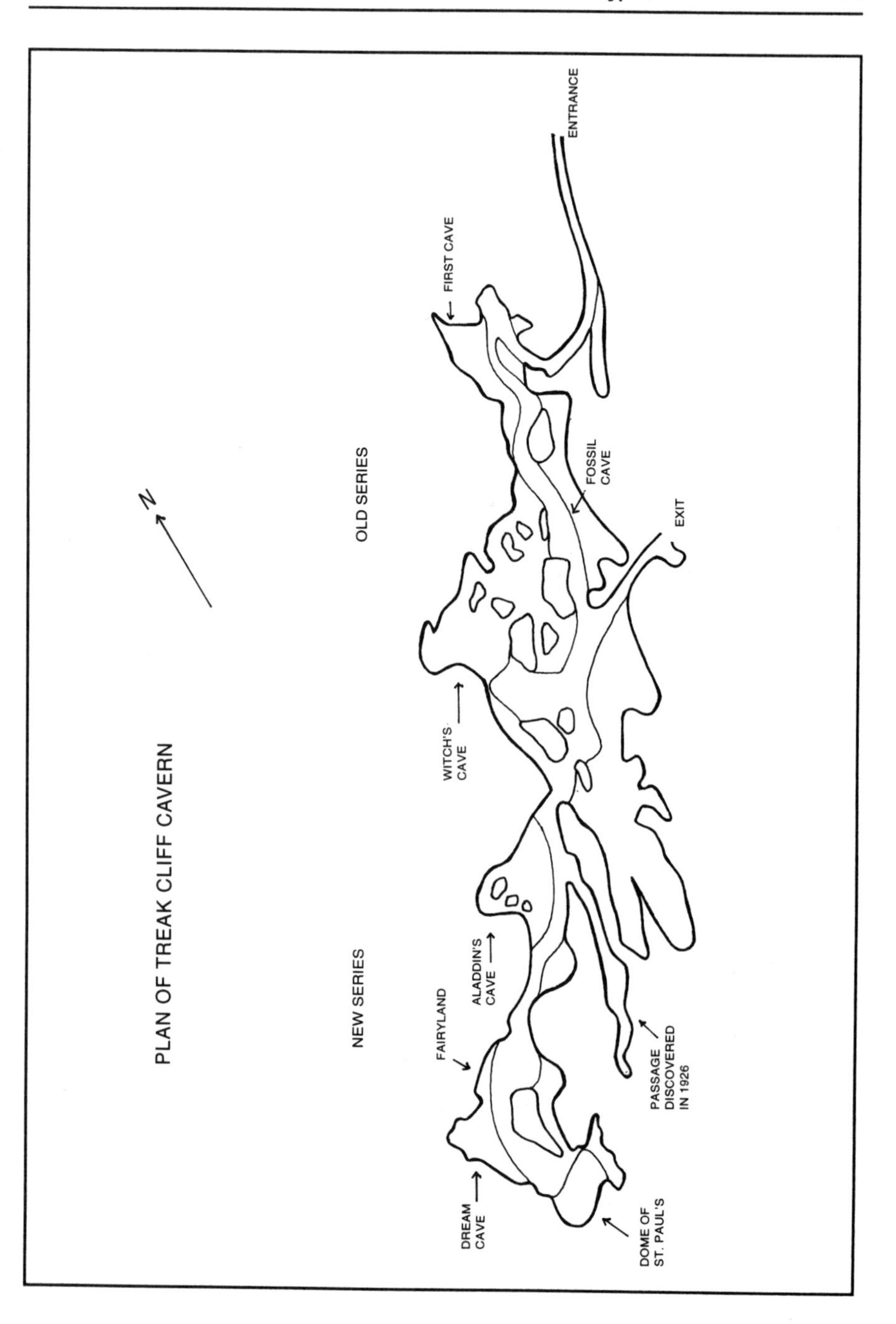
PLAN OF TREAK CLIFF CAVERN
N
OLD SERIES
NEW SERIES
ENTRANCE
FIRST CAVE
FOSSIL CAVE
EXIT
WITCH'S CAVE
ALADDIN'S CAVE
FAIRYLAND
PASSAGE DISCOVERED IN 1926
DREAM CAVE
DOME OF ST. PAUL'S

whole area was raised above sea level by earth movements and volcanic action. The rocks were twisted and fractured, and penetrated by solutions which cooled and deposited lead ore, fluorspar and other minerals. Over eons, the rock surface was eroded and streams and rivers cut into it – the process helped by the slight solubility of limestone in water. Some streams found entrances into the rock, following the lines of faults and crevices, and over further thousands of years these underground rivers, carrying boulders and debris, scoured away the rocks, forming caves. Visitors to the caves can see the evidence of this in the roofs of the caverns which are often called 'inverted river beds', the eroding and scouring effects being clearly visible. Here and there, perfectly spherical holes have been gouged out of the roofs by swirling, debris-bearing water.

The origin of the name 'Blue John' is uncertain. According to one story the mineral was given this name by two 18th-century miners, John Kirk and Joseph Hall, to distinguish it from zinc blende which was known as Black Jack. Another possibility is that the name arose in France, to where some of the mineral was exported: the rock is often of a bluish-yellow colour and French workers may have called it 'bleu-jaune' this being corrupted by the English to Blue John.

Blue John is found either in veins or in roughly spherical nodules, which are greatly prized because of their concentric rings of colour. The nodules are always embedded in clay and are not immediately recognisable except to miners. It is fairly simple to extract the nodules with hammers, crowbars and chisels, though care is needed to avoid damaging them.

Veins of Blue John are embedded in limestone and extraction of these is more difficult. The ends of the vein are found and then a deep channel is cut above its whole length. The depth of the channel to be cut can only be guess-work, as there is no way of knowing the depth of the vein. In the final stage of extraction, known as 'lifting', wedges are carefully driven beneath the deposit and the whole lump of rock is lifted and removed. The surrounding limestone is then painstakingly chiselled away, revealing the depth of the vein. It might be as much as a foot in depth, or less than an inch.

The mining of Blue John is a small-scale operation. Blasting is seldom undertaken as the shock can disturb the crystal structure of the mineral making it incapable of being worked, and may also destroy the natural bands of colour, changing the fluorspar to an opaque, off-white colour.

Nowadays the work of mining is undertaken by the cavern guides during the quiet winter months, the rock being sent down to Castleton for working and polishing.

It has often been asserted that the Romans discovered Blue John and made ornaments from it. Their settlement at Brough was only three miles from Treak Cliff, and it is possible that they came across the mineral while prospecting for lead. Vases described by the Roman scientist and philosopher Pliny are said to have been made from Blue John, and two vases made of the mineral were reportedly unearthed among the ruins of Pompeii. However, geologist Dr Trevor D Ford, who has spent many years studying Castleton's rocks and caves, is sceptical of this theory, suggesting that the Roman connection was a 19th century attempt to popularise the mineral and pointing out that the Pompeii vases were of banded amethyst.

Blue John mining began in the mid-18th century, one story concerns an employee of Earl Fitzwilliam of Wentworth who was returning home via Winnats Pass. He filled his empty wagon with stones, with the intention of constructing a rockery. Among the stones were several pieces of Blue John, and these were later noticed in the rockery by John Platt, a marble-worker from Rotherham who was visiting Wentworth. He picked out two pieces of the stone from which he made salt-cellars and these in turn came to the attention of Robert How, a Castleton geologist who was able to direct Platt to the source of the material – Treak Cliff Cavern.

This cavern consists of two distinct sections – the Old Series, which was discovered (or re-discovered) between 1745 and 1750, and the New Series, not discovered until 1926. 18th century records are vague but, by 1762, Robert Adam was decorating fireplaces in the music room of Kedleston Hall, near Derby, with Blue John. By 1765, Henry Watson, the foremost marble-worker in Derbyshire, was extracting the stone from sixteen separate mines on Treak Cliff.

The brittle nature of Blue John makes it very difficult to work. After extraction it is cleaned and stored for about a year to enable it to dry. While in this raw state, it is sawn roughly into the shape of the article to be made. It is then heated and coated with resin or shellac or, more expensively, immersed in a bath of molten resin. The resin penetrates the outer layer of crystals and binds them together, enabling the piece to be worked. When the outer layer of crystals has been removed, the process is repeated before grinding and polishing can be commenced. The earliest Blue John ornaments were relatively crude but, as a greater understanding of the stone was attained, finer works were produced, the techniques reaching a peak in the mid-19th century. One of the craftsmen's aims was to produce large items, such as bowls and vases, but to reduce the thickness of the material to a minimum so that the light would shine through it.

The industry declined towards the end of the 19th century, perhaps because of the production of similar but less expensive alabaster items, but the fluorspar was soon to be mined again in large quantities – for a very different reason.

The First World War brought a great demand for fluorspar, for use in the chemical industry and as flux in blast furnaces. In 1915, the Liverpool firm of West & Company began large-scale mining for Blue John, both in the caves and in several opencast workings on the hill above, the stone from the quarries being taken down to the road below by a small inclined railway.

In 1926, four miners were blasting close to the site of Treak Cliff Sepulchral Cave (described earlier) when they uncovered a 3ft (1m) hole leading downwards at a steep angle into a large cavern adorned with many stalactites. They climbed down into the cavity and followed its sloping floor downwards, coming across a huge hole, into the darkness of which they descended on a rope. Some 30ft (9m) below they reached the sloping floor of an enormous cavern, now known as Aladdin's Cave, the first part of Treak Cliff Cavern's New Series. The caverns leading from this were found to contain thousands of magnificent, many-coloured stalactites.

In 1932, a water-worn passage which connected the Old Series with the New was discovered, thus removing the need to descend to the latter from the hill above. Shortly after, the cavern's owner, Colonel Broadbent, entrusted John Royse, a member of one of the oldest mining families in the district, with the task of opening Treak Cliff Cavern to the public. Lighting and footpaths were installed and the cave was opened to the public at Easter, 1935. Mr Royse retired ten years later, Harold Harrison taking over his duties. His son Peter now supervises the maintenance of the cave and the small mining operation which continues there. Mr Harrison is a former Blue John miner and he makes ornaments from the mineral.

Visitors enter Treak Cliff Cavern by what is thought to have been the 18th century miners' tunnel. It is much lower and narrower today due to the addition over the years of layers of strengthening material, the tunnel having been cut through unstable clay and shale. As the tunnel progresses, however, solid rock is reached and the passage opens out, reaching, after about 32$^1/_2$yds (30m) the first cave in the Old Series. A stratum of Blue John stone known as the Cliff Blue vein is visible in the roof here, and at two points along the passageway small bowls of Blue John have been placed inside electric lamp fittings so that the light shines through, displaying the characteristic banding.

A flight of steps then leads up into the Fossil Cave where underground streams have dissolved the limestone leaving fossils protruding from the surface. The fossils are the remains of sea creatures which were alive when the limestone was being formed in the Carboniferous Period some 250 million years ago. The most common fossils here are those of crinoids or sea-lilies which, despite their name, were animals, each consisting of a 'head' resembling a sea-anemone connected by a long stalk to the sea bed. Other fossils found here include those of spirifers, which resemble cockles, and brachiopods, sometimes called lamp-shells, or Devil's Toe-nails.

The largest cavern in the Old Series is the Witch's Cave, which is 6$^1/_2$yds (approx. 6m) high, the same distance across and some 27yds (25m) long. When electric lights were being installed, a guide took a temporary extension lead and lamp up a side passage and on returning to the main cave was startled to see a large shadow, resembling a witch on a broomstick, on the cave wall. A lamp was subsequently fixed in position to maintain the effect, which is particularly appreciated by visiting school children.

From here, the passage descends to Aladdin's Cave, the first stage of the New Series, the name deriving from its rocky outcrops which resemble the stage scenery of a pantomime, backed beyond by a display of coloured stalactites. In the roof of the cave, there is a hole through which miners entered with ropes and candles in 1926. There are several stalagmites in the cave and radio-active methods of dating have established that two of them began forming about 111,000 years ago. On leaving the cavern, the visitor passes a huge boulder on which has formed a group of roughly conical stalagmites known as the Seven Dwarfs. The largest of these, 18ins (45cm) high and 8ins (20cm) wide is thought to be about 70,000 years old. The really spectacular displays are still to come, as the passage descends into the aptly named Fairyland and Dream Caves. Here, there are literally hundreds of stalactites and stalagmites of every conceivable shape and colouration, a particularly fine group in a recess in the cave's west wall having had to be protected by a metal grill from souvenir hunters. In the Dream Cave one stalactite, when viewed from the appropriate angle, bears a remarkable resemblance to a sheep's head, and attached to it is another known as The Stork. The stork's 'leg' has not quite connected with the stalagmite below it and it has been estimated that it will be a thousand years before the $1^1/_2$ inch (4cm) gap is filled.

Stalactites in the Dream Cave

The innermost cave in Treak Cliff Cavern is the "Dome of St Paul's", some 12yds (11m) high and $8^1/_2$yds (8m) wide, the walls of which have been richly coloured by the mineral-laden water seeping into the cave. The presence of iron is shown by reds, oranges and browns; that of copper by blues and greens, and manganese by a purple hue. It is likely that the cavern reaches yet further into the hillside, containing who knows what geological marvels, but the passage is blocked by a huge limestone boulder. This could be blasted away, but the shock would destroy the cavern's stalactite displays.

Treak Cliff Cavern is the most attractive of the Castleton show caves, and the easiest through which to walk.

Blue John Cavern

It is possible that the Romans were the first to enter Blue John Cavern, though the mineral has probably only been mined here since about 1770. Blue John Cavern was opened to the public as early as 1800, improvements being undertaken in about 1843. Visitors enter the cavern today by means of a short flight of steps followed by a man-made passage some 20ft (6m) long. This leads into a natural cave which contains the Roman Level and the Five Vein workings. The route now follows the course of a natural passage, carved out of the rock by water and into which the miners built winding stone steps.

At the bottom of the steps the passage follows the course of an ancient underground river, the river bed having been filled and levelled by the miners using spoil from the workings. The passages here are very smooth and, looking upwards, one can see round holes cut into the roof by swirling water. In the side of the passageway, there is an excavation known as The Bull Beef Working. The name comes from the reddish meat-like colouration of the Blue John stone here and it is from this vein that some of the largest, most colourful pieces of the mineral have come. Chatsworth House and the library of The Vatican in Rome contain vases made from Bull Beef stone and one enormous piece was used to make what might be the finest Blue John ornament known. This is a table constructed by the Woodruff family of Buxton, the table top beautifully marked by concentric rings of colour and just under 3ft 6ins (approx. 1m) across – being supported by an ormolu base. The table is thought to be worth in the region of half a million pounds and is part of the Ollerenshaw Collection on view at the Cavendish House Museum in Castleton.

The passage leads into the Crystallised Cavern, which has a high dome-shaped roof and walls spectacularly coloured with crystals and minerals. Here, in the 19th century, a large chandelier bearing many candles was hoisted to roof height using a windlass to display the beauties of the cave to visitors. The chandelier was last used in the 1840s and was long assumed to have been lost. However, in 1959, during improvement work, it was discovered wedged high in the rocks, together with a large metal pan. This was filled with a mixture known as Bengal Light which was ignited by guides to give visitors a better view of the cave. The chandelier can be seen today in the cavern, with the remains of the windlass.

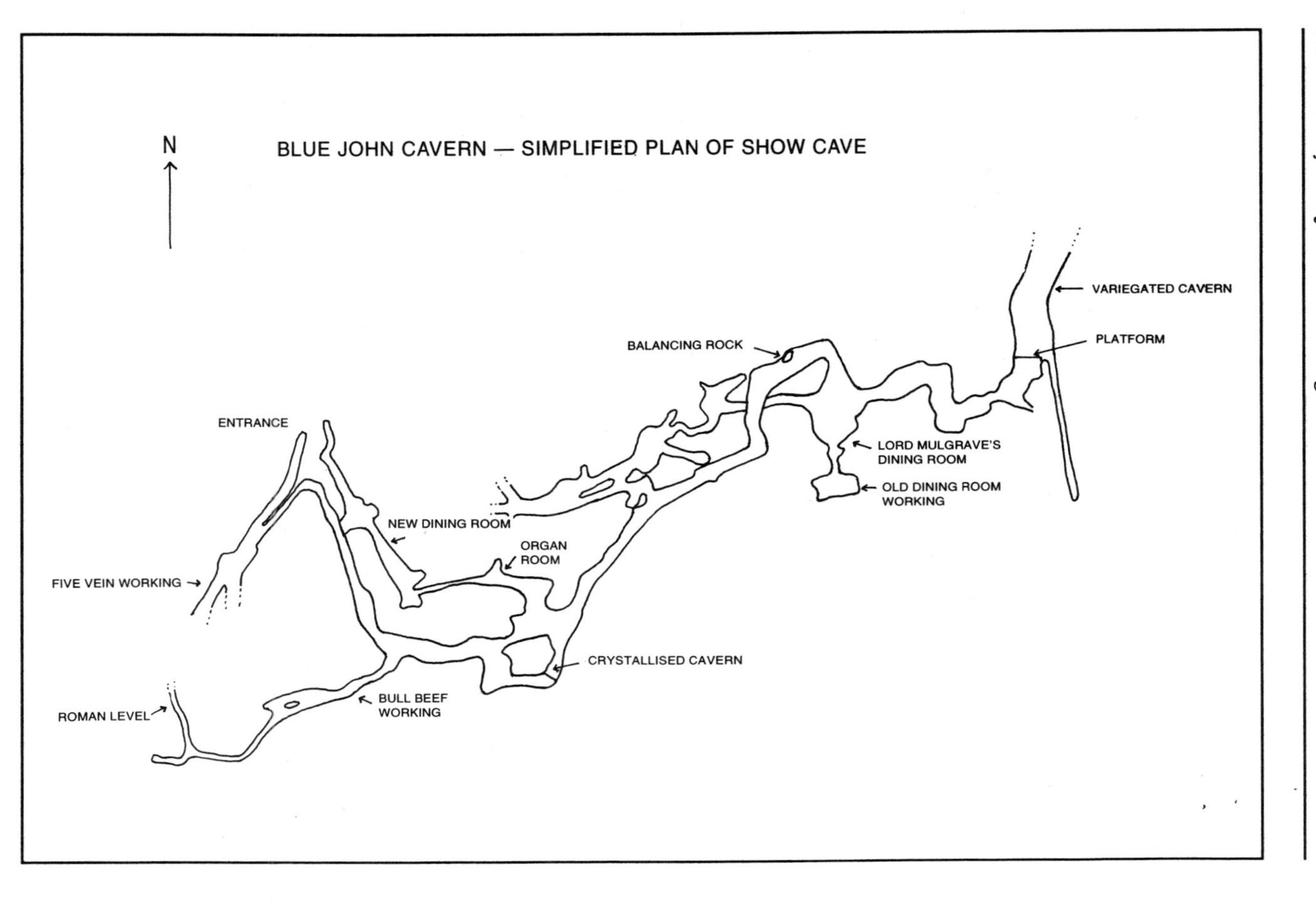
N
BLUE JOHN CAVERN — SIMPLIFIED PLAN OF SHOW CAVE
VARIEGATED CAVERN
PLATFORM
BALANCING ROCK
LORD MULGRAVE'S DINING ROOM
OLD DINING ROOM WORKING
ENTRANCE
NEW DINING ROOM
ORGAN ROOM
FIVE VEIN WORKING
CRYSTALLISED CAVERN
ROMAN LEVEL
BULL BEEF WORKING

The passage now leads into the Waterfall Cavern, so named from a beautiful formation of stalagmites which covers one wall and which resembles a frozen, multi-coloured waterfall, dripping over the rocky ledges. It is further enhanced by delicate horizontal ribbing. The next notable feature is the Stalactite Cavern, whose name is self-explanatory, the passageway then leading into Lord Mulgrave's Dining Room. The cavern is roughly circular and was created by the confluence of two underground rivers which formed a vast whirlpool, the upper level of which has left a horizontal mark on the cavern walls. The cave is named after a benevolent aristocrat who is said to have treated the miners to a banquet here. On one side of the cave can be seen the Blue John vein known as the Dining Room Level.

The water-excavated passageway now leads into the Variegated Cavern which is some 200ft (60m) high and whose walls are coloured with various minerals. An impressive display of stalagmites adorns one wall and, in a cleft in the rock wall facing the visitors' platform, is a beautiful cream-coloured 'curtain' stalactite. Beyond the platform, the cavern is covered with huge boulders which the subterranean river tore out of the cave walls and carried down here. The power of the river is well demonstrated by a huge boulder, whose weight is estimated at two tons, which is wedged into a cleft in the rocks. The Variegated Cavern marks the end of the show cave.

Other features of note are the Organ Room (see plan) where a formation of connecting stalactites and stalagmites resembled a series of organ pipes (sadly destroyed by blasting many years ago) and the passage leading from this to the New Dining Room working. The passage contains a deposit of crinoid marble, formed when the remains of crinoids, or sea-lilies, were compacted by heat and pressure, the mineral being used to make ornamental pieces of furniture such as table tops.

It should be pointed out that there are about 250 steps in the Blue John Mine and climbing back up these to leave the cavern is a laborious process. A notice above the entrance to the cave warns that the journey is not suitable for people who have heart problems.

LEAD MINING

The Old Man

For almost two thousand years lead mining was a major industry in the limestone country of Derbyshire, the mining field extended roughly from Castleton in the north to Wirksworth in the south, from Buxton in the west to Matlock in the east. The casual visitor to the county might see little evidence of the industry today, but strike off the beaten track and look carefully and the signs are there: old shafts covered with railway sleepers or stone cairns; patches of hillocky, disturbed ground; the remains of small stone buildings or *coes*, where the miners kept their tools, and the masonry of an engine house, half obscured by a clump of trees. In a few locations considerably more of the industry can be seen, such as the Magpie Mine, near Sheldon, where the buildings and winding gear are well-preserved, and the Good Luck Mine, near Middleton-by-Wirksworth where visitors can descend – supervised – into parts of the old workings. The Derbyshire lead miner has been referred to for centuries as the 'Old Man', this term also being applied to parts of a lead mine which have been worked in years gone by.

Lead was almost certainly mined in Derbyshire before the arrival of the Romans in 45 AD, but it is only with their occupation that we find definite evidence of the industry. This includes smelting hearths, such as that discovered near Duffield, and lead ingots, or pigs, bearing Latin inscriptions. One such pig was stamped with the name of the Emperor Hadrian (76 – 138 AD) while others were inscribed with the names of less illustrious officials. It has been suggested that pigs bearing the emperor's name were destined for the Roman treasury, while the others were used in ordinary transactions. Some Derbyshire ingots bear the letters LVTVD, thought to be an abbreviation of Lutudarum. This might have been the Roman name for a settlement at Matlock, near to where some of the pigs were found, or it could have been the Latin term for the lead-mining area of Derbyshire. Several lead mines such as the Masson Mine at Matlock Bath, are said to be of Roman origin, but although some very archaic-looking workings have been found it is hard to establish their date. Roman coins are said to have been found in some mines, including those of Deep Rake (with a traditionally Roman origin), Elton Moor and Crich, though details of these finds are vague.

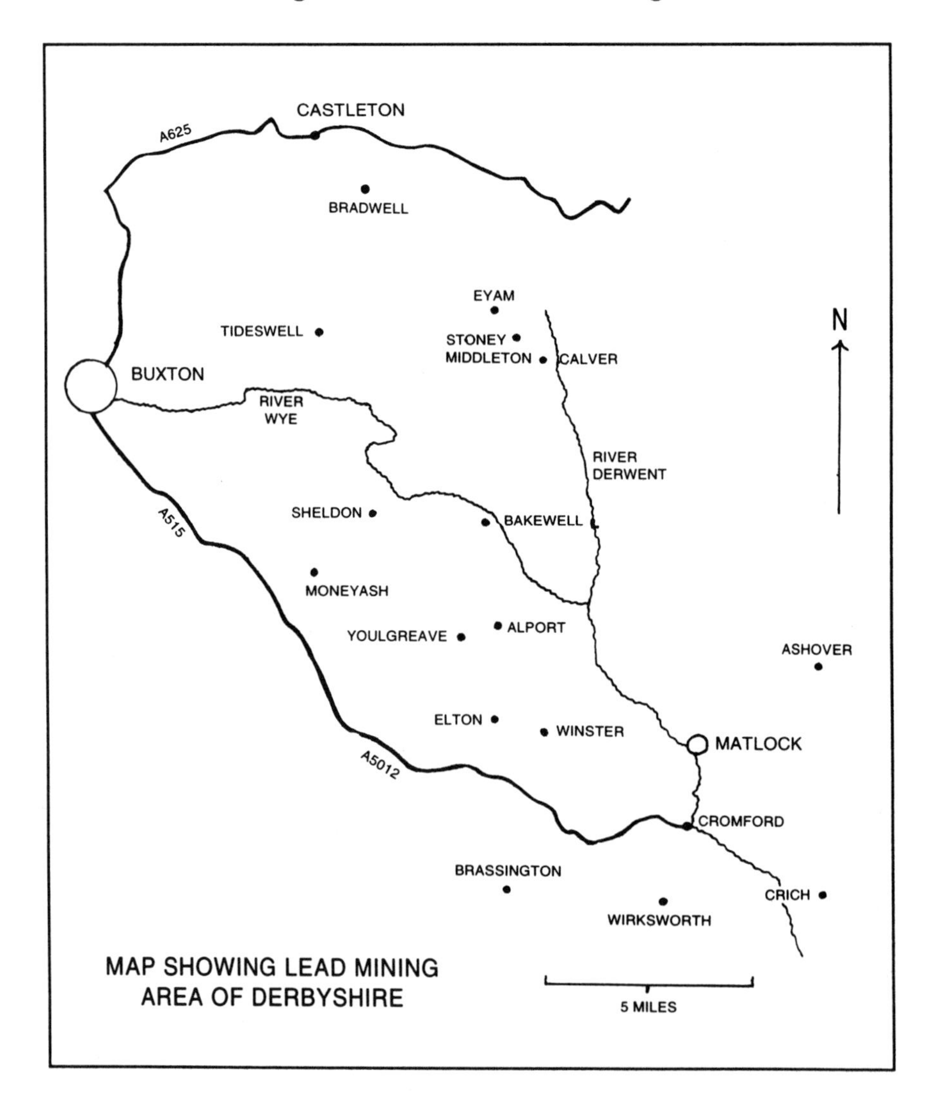

MAP SHOWING LEAD MINING AREA OF DERBYSHIRE

The mining of lead seems to have declined in Derbyshire after the Roman withdrawal, but to have revived with the coming of the Saxons and Danes. The industry expanded during the medieval period and the 16th and 17th centuries, stimulated by the use of lead in house and church building. Vast quantities of the metal were used in the building of great houses such as Derbyshire's Haddon and Hardwick Halls, on the roofs, as gutters and downspounts, in cisterns and pipes and in windows. Lead mining reached a peak during the 18th century with the sinking of ever deeper shafts, the driving of extensive drainage tunnels or soughs, the use of steam pumping-engines and the investment of outside capital. The industry suffered mixed fortunes in the 19th century, new uses were continually being found for the metal and some very rich deposits were found but by 1830 lead ore was being imported from abroad, notably from Spain. Investment declined and prices fell, the final blow coming in the 1880s with the importing of very cheap lead ore from Australia. Only a few mines survived into the 20th century, the last of these closing in the 1960s and today lead is only mined in Britain as a by-product of other minerals.

The laws and customs surrounding Derbyshire lead mining are ancient and complex and only a very simplified description can be given here. Following their invasion of England in 874, the Danes seized control of the Wirksworth lead mines, declaring them to be the property of their king, Ceowulf. From now on, this area was known as the King's Field, all its mineral rights belonging to the Crown. By the King's Field, several smaller lead-mining areas, or Liberties, came into existence, the manorial rights of each belonging to one or more landowners and each having its own laws and customs, similar to those of the King's Field.

For centuries it had been an almost unquestioned right of the miners to dig for lead wherever they thought it might lie, but this brought them increasingly into conflict with private landowners who tried to sue them for trespass. The conflict reached a head during the reign of Edward I, who ordered an enquiry which was held at Ashbourne in 1288, and the outcome was the setting down in writing, for the first time, of the laws governing the mining of lead. The Code, as it was called, had a special status, remaining outside ordinary English law until the 19th century when it was modified and made statutory by the Mineral Acts for Derbyshire Mines of 1851 and 1852, in which the essentials of the early Code were largely retained.

This established the right of any man to dig for lead at will, unhindered by the landowner or leaseholder. The only places exempt from this were churchyards, gardens, orchards and the King's Highway, though tunnelling could proceed beneath these. The ruling gave the miner virtual freedom from the Law of Trespass, remarkable in a country where a man's estate was regarded as almost sacrosanct. It is still not certain why such a freedom was granted, though it might have been simply to encourage the growth of the industry. Lead was an important commodity for the country, providing valuable exports and, of course, constant revenue for the Crown.

The Code also directed that, should a miner discover ore, the landowner had to allow him access to water and to a road, and to provide him with land for a coe and spoilheaps.

The mining Code was administered by the Barmote or Barmoot Courts, each Liberty having its own court. They were held twice a year, each consisting of a jury of from twelve to twenty-four members who held office until the next court. Permanent officials were the Steward or Clerk of the Court and the Barmaster. The latter was an important and powerful figure, supervising the everyday administration of the Code, dispensing justice and, up to the Mining Acts of the 19th century, even acting as coroner at mining fatalities.

One of the most important functions of the Barmaster was to establish the validity of a new claim. A miner asserted his right to dig by marking the spot with a cross cut in the ground. He then set up his stow, which was a simple winch made from wood – curiously, iron nails or bolts were forbidden. This had to be done within a few days and the Barmaster informed. If there were no counter claims the miner then had nine weeks in which to produce two dishes of ore. A dish equalled 14 Winchester pints, as laid down by the Standard Dish which hangs in the Moot Hall at Wirksworth, and which was presented to the miners by King Henry VIII. Every three weeks, the Barmaster cut a nick in the winding gear, to remind the miner of the passage of time. If no ore was forthcoming after three nicks the claim was disallowed, leaving it free for anyone else wishing to try his luck.

Much of the Barmaster's time was spent in trying to disentangle the often incredibly complex disputes of the miners. Arguments frequently arose over the ownership of a particular vein of lead, while another common cause of dispute was the driving of drainage soughs. A sough dug to drain one working, for example, might then flood another. One case, that of Stoke Sough on the Eyam field, was apparently beyond the ability of the Barmaster to settle, for it was sent to Chancery where it dragged on for 23 years! Often Barmasters and members of the Barmote Juries, in cases of dispute, had to descend into the workings to obtain what they called a *View*. If their way was blocked, with waste stone, for example, they would order the removal of 'the Obstruction of the Old Man'.

It was obviously essential for the miners themselves to have some knowledge of the mining laws, but most were illiterate. In 1653, to help overcome this, Edward Manlove, the Steward of the Wirksworth Barmote Court, published the Code in a doggerel poem. It was easily learned and helped many generations of Derbyshire lead miners.

The Mines

Lead most commonly occurs as galena, or lead sulphide, a crystalline substance which varies in colour from steely grey to a bright blue. A less common source is cerussite or lead carbonate, known as white lead and long used in the manufacture of paint. Galena is often found with zinc and iron ore and with minerals such as quartz, calcite, fluorite and barite. Lead deposits are found in three main types of vein known as rakes, flats and pipes. Rakes extend up to 60ft (18m) in width, may descend vertically for hundreds of feet and run a length of several miles. Pipe veins are roughly cylindrical in shape, being a filling of old underground passages and can be enormous – a pipe-working in a cavern discovered at Crich, near Belper, in 1828 was estimated to contain a thousand tons of almost pure galena. Flat veins lie in roughly horizontal layers between beds of rock and though they may extend over a wide area are usually only a few inches thick.

In the earliest days of lead mining the ore was worked only where a vein could be seen at the surface, shallow galleries being dug into the ground. As surface deposits were worked-out, however, and as mining techniques improved, deep shafts were sunk. Sometimes these had to pass through soft ground before reaching solid rock and they were then lined with masonry, or ginged, as the miners termed the process. This was usually done with blocks of the local limestone, sometimes as rough boulders, sometimes as dressed bricks, though the shafts of the mines worked at Winster by the London Lead Company were ginged with curved blocks of gritstone. Mortar was not used, except in the most recent of shafts, and in all but the largest mines the work was done by the miners themselves. On Eyam Edge some shafts had to be ginged for a depth of about 500ft (150m) before the ore-bearing rock was reached. From the base of the shaft, passages or 'gates' as they were called, were driven along the veins.

The smaller lead mines had only one shaft, used both for ascent and descent, and raising the ore, but the larger workings had two or more. Climbing shafts were usually about 2ft (0.6m) across with bars of wood called stemples being driven at intervals of about 2ft (0.6m) into alternate sides of the shaft to form a primitive ladder. Sometimes projecting stones were used instead of wood, and in some workings footholds were simply cut into the walls of the shaft. Ladders made of wood, iron and chain did not come into use until the early 19th century. The deeper climbing shafts were sometimes divided by platforms.

A winding or drawing shaft, up which the ore was raised to the surface was usually wider, perhaps 6ft (1.75m) across and at its base was a flat space known as a bridging floor where the bridger loaded the ore into containers known as corves to be lifted out. A larger mine might have a series of horizontal shafts or levels, connected by vertical sumps, the ore being lifted from one level to the next by means of a stow, or windlass.

Corves, or kibbles as they were sometimes called, were about 2ft (0.6m) deep and a foot (0.3m) across. Sometimes they were made of wooden staves bound with iron hoops, sometimes made completely of wrought iron. In medieval times leather bags were used, and these have sometimes been discovered in old workings. Stows were used in the earliest days to lift corves to the surface, but in the 17th century horse-gins came into use (see picture). Steam engines came into use in the 18th century but do not seem to have been used to any great extent for lifting the ore, their main purpose being to pump water out of the mines. Ropes were used in the earliest gins, chains coming into use in the mid-19th century. The ropes were often made locally – at Monyash, Elton and in the gaping entrance of Peak Cavern at Castleton where the remains of rope-making equipment, still used in this century, can be seen. The gin ropes were often hundreds of feet long, as much as $1^{1}/_{2}$ins (4cm) thick and 5ins (12cm) in circumference.

Miners used picks, wedges and chisels to cut into the rock, often cracking and softening it first by lighting fires against it; this method was used in Derbyshire until well into the 19th century. A primitive type of blasting using quicklime was also used, the quicklime being inserted into holes bored into the rock, which were then sealed with wooden bungs. Water was then poured into holes bored through the bungs and the violent reaction of the water and quicklime split the rock. The use of gunpowder for blasting seems first to have been used in England in the 17th century, but blasting methods were slow to catch on, perhaps because the process of drilling holes in the rock, which needed two men, one holding the drill and turning it while the other struck it with a heavy hammer, was difficult in the cramped workings of the lead mines. Illumination was provided by candles, fixed at suitable points in the tunnel walls or attached by lumps of clay to the miners' hats.

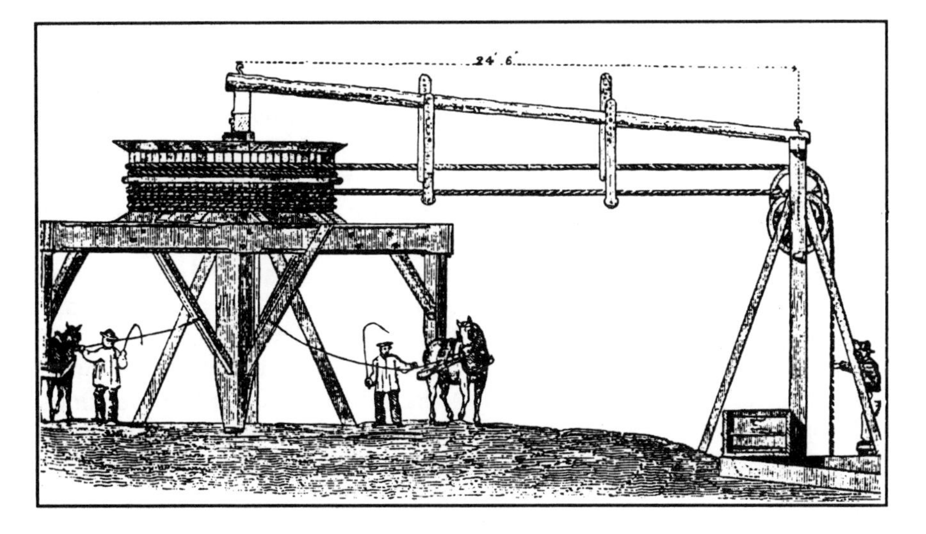

A horse gin

This method of working was known as stoping – working in steps. The older method was underhand stoping, the miner driving downwards and throwing ore and waste upwards onto platforms called *bunnings*, which were fixed across the tunnels. In overhand stoping, introduced in the 19th century, the miners bored horizontally or upwards, throwing ore and waste downwards, the ore being transported to the base of the drawing shaft on sledges or in wagons.

Early tunnels were usually very small, sometimes only about 3ft (approx. 1m) high and 2ft (0.6m) wide. An interesting variation is the coffin-gate or coffin-level, this resembling in cross-section a coffin, being narrow at the top, then widening out before tapering to the floor. A particularly good example of this was discovered at the Ball Eye Mine near Cromford, where a coffin-level between 4ft and 5ft (1.2m and 1.5m) high was driven for hundreds of feet. The date of this tunnel is uncertain – it might be pre-18th century. Some of the later Derbyshire mines were vast, such as Middleton Mine near Youlgreave, first worked for lead and later for calcite. Nellie Kirkham described the mine as it appeared in the 1950s in her book *Derbyshire Lead Mining through the Centuries* (1968):

'The 300ft level ranged in a straight line for over 2,000ft to the west and over 1,000ft to the east along the sole of a worked-out rake vein, which was 60ft or so wide, and about 80ft to 100ft high. The vein stuff was calcite which was being worked commercially. At the west end the face sloped upwards in a bank of calcite, etc., looking like scree with a miner drilling at the top, 50ft or so above, silhouetted against the speck of his light. It was very beautiful, dimly lit, slightly smoky from the blasting, with the roof a dusky darkness beyond the reach of light. In its great open-ness, this mine appeared to be more like a huge cavern than most lead mines, with a vast and misty beauty of greys and blacks.'

Another huge lead mine, perhaps the most productive in the British Isles, was the Mill Close Mine at Darley Dale. This had been worked intermittently since the 17th century and mining was just about to cease again when, in about 1860, a particularly rich vein was discovered. The vein ran in a northerly and then north-westerly direction, the mine finally reaching a point about 3ml (4.75km) from the earliest workings and some 1000ft (300m) below ground. The vein often led into huge caverns where exceptionally pure lead ore was found as huge boulders embedded in sand and clay. Zinc-blende was also discovered, one cavern, 400ft (120m) long and 20ft (6m) wide, being lined with the substance which was covered with huge calcite crystals a foot (30cm) long. One vein, sandwiched between an upper bed of clay and a lower bed of limestone, contained thousands of tons of lead ore. Between 1861 and its closure in 1958 the mine yielded over half a million tons of lead concentrates and over 90,000 tons of zinc.

Visitors should take great care when exploring lead mining areas of the countryside. Many old shafts still exist, some perhaps uncapped, and the ground close to these could be unstable.

Water in the Workings

In time, as the lead mines were sunk deeper, the difficulties increased, the main problem being the water which poured into the workings from the saturated terrain. This could sometimes be channelled away through caves and natural outlets, but other methods were often needed. Primitive hand-pumps were used and water was also lifted out in leather buckets attached to ropes and raised with a windlass. Horse gins were sometimes used to raise water, and another method was the 'rag and chain' pump which consisted of a vertical barrel or pipe through which was passed an endless chain fitted at intervals with leather discs or bags filled with rags (see illustration). These fitted snugly in the walls of the pipe and as the chain was turned the water was carried to the surface in the several compartments. They were often used in series and in Derbyshire at least were worked manually.

By the 17th century, however, such methods were completely inadequate and to overcome the problems, underground channels known as soughs were dug to allow the water to drain off. These were often remarkable excavations in their own right, being dug by specialised workers contracted to mine owners. They could be several miles in length and required careful planning and excavating. Some soughs were as much as 8ft (2.5m) high and 9ft (2.75m) wide. They usually descended from the main shaft to their outlet at a gradient of 10ft (3m) in a mile (1.6km) though steeper slopes were sometimes necessary. Excavated material had to be pulled up shafts, carried out in wagons or floated out on boats. Where soughs were excavated through unstable ground they had to be roofed and lined with masonry, the stones of the arched roof being wedge-shaped so that pressure from the ground above would pack them firmly. A sough's outflow would usually be finished with a semi-circular brick arch. In some, the masonry is still in excellent condition a hundred or two hundred years after construction. Sometimes soughs, or sections of them, were used as passages by miners and in such cases stone or wooden channels were built along the sides to carry the water. The longer ones required ventilation, this being provided by fans, bellows and air-shafts. One hundred and fifty soughs are known to have been excavated, at least six passing beneath the town of Wirksworth. The earliest known was dug in the 1630s though there must previously have been very short channels made to connect a working with a river or stream.

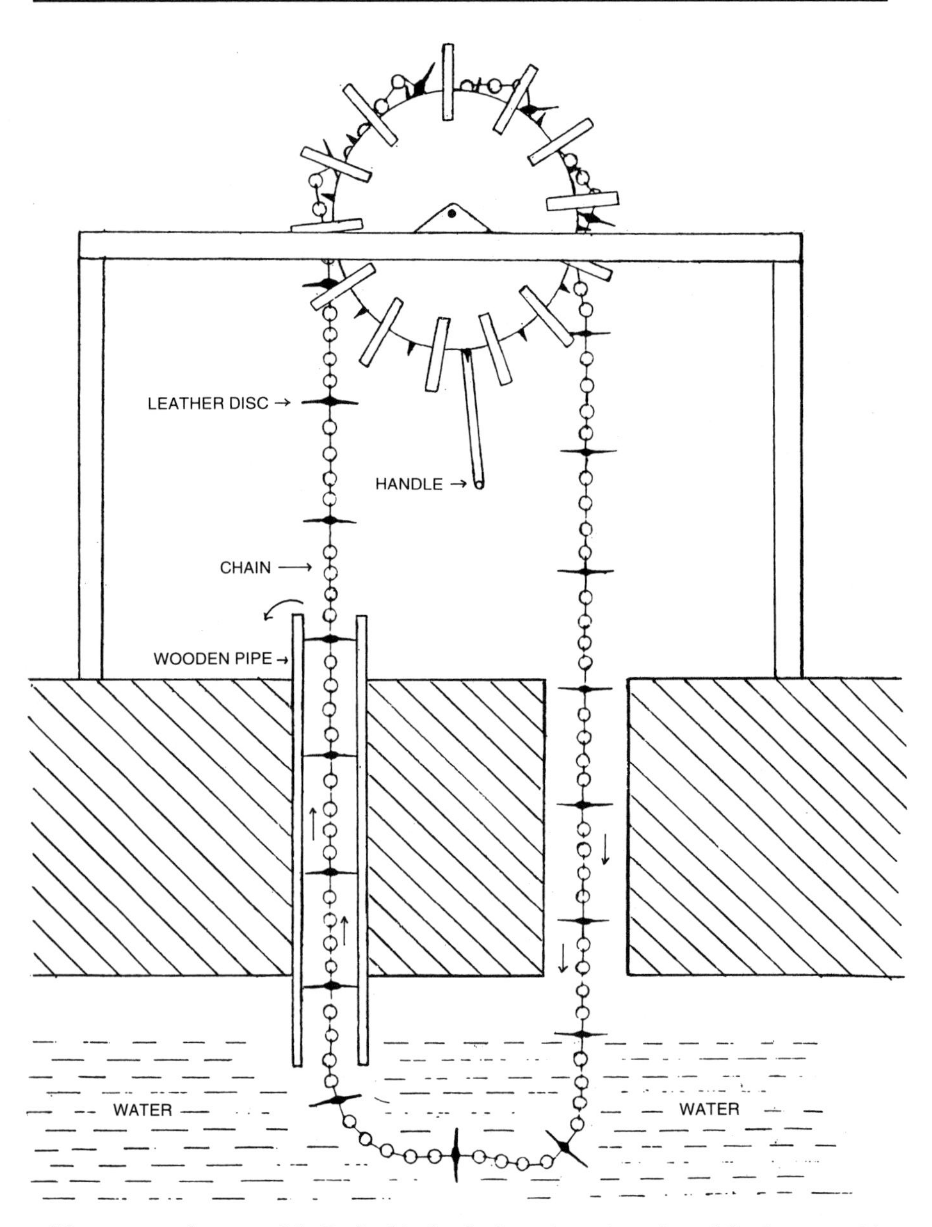

Water-pump of type used in Derbyshire lead mines. Sometimes, bags full of rags would be used instead of the leather discs illustrated here

Soughs were difficult and dangerous to construct. They often had to be driven through solid rock by men working by candle-light. Besides the obvious hazards of tunnelling work there was danger when they ran through shales, from explosive gases such as methane and hydrogen sulphide, known as fire-damp. A more frequent hazard which could arise anywhere along them was choke-damp or carbon dioxide. The longer soughs took years to construct, even with the use of gunpowder, and they remain a testament to the determination and tenacity of their builders.

The mines, however, went even deeper and even soughs became inadequate to drain them. By now, though, steam power was being developed. In 1705 Thomas Newcomen patented his atmospheric pumping engine, and ten years later a Newcomen engine was installed to pump out the water at Yatestoop mine at Winster, near Matlock. Steam technology was improved in the late-18th century by Boulton and Watt and in the early 19th century by Richard Trevithick and larger and more sophisticated engines began to appear in the lead mines. They were often called Cornish engines, much of the technology having been developed in that county for tin mining. The 200 horse-power engine used at Calver Sough Mine and later sold to the Magpie Mine was built at Bowling Iron Works in Bradford in 1858. Parts of Derbyshire came to resemble the tin-mining areas of Cornwall, studded as they were with a similar type of tall-chimneyed engine-house.

Despite such technological advances, though, earlier methods of draining the mines continued to be used, including pumps worked by water wheels such as the 52ft (15.5m) diameter wheel installed at the Lathkill Dale vein in 1836, and soughs. Sometimes soughs performed a dual function – drainage and the carrying of ore and waste out of the mine. The longest sough in Derbyshire was the Hillcarr Sough, near Alport, unusual in that it was built to drain several veins and mines rather than just one. It was constructed between 1766 and 1787, cost the lives of six men – killed in a firedamp explosion – and was $2^1/_2$ml (4km) long. Extensions were added to the sough as late as 1882 bringing its total length to about 4ml (6.3km).

Another impressive sough was that dug as late as 1873 – 1881 to drain the Magpie Mine at Sheldon. The mine had previously been drained by a Newcomen engine, installed in 1824 and then in 1868 by the Bowling Iron Works machine already mentioned. The cost of the coal for the latter, however, was considered exorbitant, so it was decided to drive a sough from the south bank of the River Wye, underneath the village of Sheldon, to the main shaft, a distance of about $1^1/_4$ml (2km). The sough is the only one in Derbyshire, apparently, where drilling machines were used. In 1874 the company installed a water wheel at the sough's entrance to work a rock drill, this being replaced four years later by percussion drills of the type designed by the engineer Richard Schram, which were powered by compressed air. The sough met the shaft at a depth below ground of 579ft (174m) there still being a further 200ft (60m) of shaft below this level. The steam engine, though, could easily and cheaply raise the water from these depths to the entrance of the sough. Soughs and engines were used in conjunction like this in several lead mines. The Magpie sough was driven through solid rock and was 6ft to 8ft high (1.75m to 2.5m) and 7ft to 9ft wide (2m to 2.75m). It was fitted with lock gates to control water levels and carried boats full of ore. When the mine was re-worked for zinc blende at the beginning of the 20th century the boats used for this purpose were each about 24ft (7.25m) long and 4ft (1.25m) wide and carried up to 50 cwt of ore. Pot-holing groups occasionally explore soughs, but only experienced and well-equipped teams should enter them.

Stone-work in Hillcarr Sough

The Lead Miner

What sort of men were the lead miners? Physically they were very tough, their work being hard and dangerous. Much of the tunnelling was accomplished with sheer muscle power using picks and wedges and, even when blasting powder was used, there was the laborious process of boring shot holes with hammers and drills. Then there were the arduous tasks of loading and transporting the ore underground. Daniel Defoe described meeting a lead miner (the occupant of Harborough Cave) who had just climbed up a narrow shaft with his tools and three-quarters of a hundredweight (38kg) of lead ore from a depth of 360ft (108m), the miner describing how some of his colleagues were working a further 100ft (30m) below him.

Early lead miners seem to have dressed in leather, as did the miner encountered by Defoe, who also wore a brimless leather cap. In the 19th century canvas trousers and flannel clothes and caps appeared and a later development was the felt hat called a Bradder. Candles were often affixed to head gear with lumps of clay. Smoking seems to have been universal among lead miners, their pipes, of all shapes and sizes and dating from Elizabethan times, having been found in old workings and spoil heaps. They were often afflicted by respiratory complaints and from rheumatism caused by the cramped, wet conditions but surprisingly they do not appear to have suffered greatly from lead poisoning and many lived to a ripe old age: Nellie Kirkham writes:

'One fact of interest which emerges from a 1614 lead ore tithe suit is the longevity of the miners. A number were over eighty, others in their seventies, while sixty was a common age'.

In the early days of lead mining the miners worked on a self-employed basis, often forming small gangs and making agreements with the agents or owners of mines about how much they should be paid per load of ore. Usually they would provide their own candles, gunpowder and so on, but occasionally these were supplied by the mine owners. With the development of larger mines, more lead miners worked for wages, usually for shifts of eight hours, or six in wet weather. Relations between owners and miners were usually amicable. Records from the larger mines show that men were paid when flooding stopped them from working; they would be supplied with ale, meat and bread on special occasions such as New Year's Day and the Miners' Holiday in May and were often given provisions during hard times. In the smaller companies miners often benefited by being shareholders.

Miners' wives often worked at the surface, dressing the ore (very occasionally women worked underground) and mining families would often grow their own oats and vegetables and rear a few animals. They often lived rent free or paid a nominal sum and could take stone and clay without payment from parish quarries and clay-pits. It was not an easy life but lead miners seem to have had more freedom and better conditions than many other early industrial workers.

The miners were a pugnacious breed who often had a great sense of personal attachment to their mines, many families having mined lead for generations. They would fight bitterly for their rights and this could lead to loss of life as occurred at Magpie Mine in 1833. The trouble had begun in 1824 when tunnels from the Magpie and the adjacent Red Soil Mine ran close together, the men from each mine being firmly convinced that a particular section of vein was theirs. The dispute continued for several years with fights underground, the vandalising of each other's workings and the continual involvement of the Barmote Court. It probably did not help matters that some of the Magpie men and the mine agent were Cornish, while most of the Red Soil miners were local. The complex dispute reached a tragic climax on an August day in 1833.

The Red Soil men took straw down their mine which they set fire to in an attempt to drive the Magpie miners away from the disputed area. The latter retaliated next day by burning straw, sulphur and petroleum, driving the Red Soil men to the surface, after which the latter's overseer covered the shaft openings, hoping perhaps to drive the fumes back into the Magpie Mine. Next day, the Red Soil miners went below, not realising that the workings were full of toxic fumes. Shortly after, several half-suffocated men struggled to the surface leaving others below. A rescue attempt was immediately mounted, the men from both mines joining forces, but despite their efforts three men died of asphyxiation. Subsequently, seventeen of the Magpie Miners were charged with murder, their case being heard at the Derby Assizes in 1834 but the facts of the case were hard to disentangle and the Magpie men pleaded that they had only been defending their rights. They were acquitted.

The industry was rich in superstition and folklore. Like the Cornish tin miners the Derbyshire lead miners believed in the Knockers, elves or dwarfs whose hammers could be heard tapping deep in the workings. In Bradwell, when the miners went home on Christmas Eve they left half a candle burning for the Old Man and it was considered bad luck to work in the mines on Good Friday. For centuries dowsing rods were used to find ore and a story from the 18th century relates that when a pumping engine at Calver did not work properly the miners laid rowan branches on it, hoping to counteract the witchcraft which they believed had stopped it functioning, a strange mixture of technology and superstition! If a miner were overcome by choke damp – carbon dioxide – he would be brought to the surface where a patch of turf would be removed and the man laid down with his face in the soil in the belief that this would increase his chance of recovery. Damp, cloudy weather, particularly if associated with trees in bud, was believed to increase the risk of choke-damp.

Lead miners were great believers in the importance of dreams and rich veins were often said to have been found after their whereabouts were vouchsafed in dreams. Dreams were also said to foretell danger and a mine owner once ordered his men out of the workings following a vivid dream of disaster. Later that day, the mine shaft collapsed. On another occasion, a mine owner who had decided to sell his mine believed that he had heard a voice in his mine repeatedly whispering "there's ore". He gave no credence to this and sold the mine, and the new owner immediately discovered a rich vein. A belief which persisted into very recent times was that it was unlucky to whistle underground; Nellie Kirkham was told by a lead miner that one day, when a lad, he had whistled in the mine and was threatened by a furious old miner with his hammer.

Deserted lead mines were often said to be haunted, including the Magpie Mine at Sheldon, where the ghosts were said to be those of the Red Soil men who had been killed in the 1830s. The mine had an evil reputation for a long time after, various disasters occurring there. The mine closed in 1926, being taken over by the Peak District Mines Historical Society in 1962, and in the first five years there was a roof fall, a flood and a fire. It was said that if you stood at the top of the old shaft you could hear the ghostly voices of the long-dead miners calling in the galleries below and, in 1946, a group exploring the old workings reported seeing and photographing a ghost. David Clark, in his *Ghosts and Legends of the Peak District* (1991), described how one of the explorers:

'...reported that he had seen a man with a candle walking along a tunnel from which he had disappeared without trace. A photograph of another member of the party on a raft in a sough at the mine showed a second man standing, apparently, on 9ft of water.'

The workings of Sallet Hole Mine near Stoney Middleton are said to be haunted by a figure wearing a long coat and cap who disappears into thin air. A ghost known as 'th' owd man' is said to haunt the old fluorspar workings at Hanging Flatt Mine near Eyam. He wanders around with a spade on his shoulder muttering to himself and oblivious to onlookers. A lady who lived at a farm close to the mine told author Clarence Daniel that she had heard the strokes of a pick within the mine although it was closed at the time.

Another type of phantom said to haunt old workings, was a huge black dog which was considered a portent of disaster. One night a Bradwell miner was returning home with a friend when he saw a gigantic black dog which walked slowly up to them and vanished at their feet. The miner repeatedly drew his friend's attention to the dog but his companion could not see it. The miner who saw the apparition considered it an omen and would not go down the mine next day. His friend however insisted on going down as usual and was killed when the roof fell in.

A group of Derbyshire lead miners, early 20th century

THE CRESWELL DISASTER: FIRE DOWN BELOW

The Fire

The deepest tunnels that man drives underground are probably those used for the mining of coal. It is inevitably a hazardous undertaking and the history of mining is a grim one, many appalling underground accidents having occurred. The counties of Derbyshire and Nottinghamshire have not been spared such tragedies – indeed, what may be the first recorded mining fatality occurred in Derby in 1291 when a miner was struck and killed by a falling basket of coal. One of the worst accidents in English mining history occurred at Creswell Colliery on 26th September 1950, when eighty men lost their lives.

Creswell Colliery is in north-east Derbyshire, close to its border with Nottinghamshire, being some 6ml (9.5km), to the south-west of Worksop. Before the nationalisation of the mines in 1947, it was owned by the Bolsover Colliery Company Ltd. The mine has two circular shafts, each 18ft (5.5m) in diameter, which were completed in 1896. These were sunk to reach the Top Hard seam at a depth of 1330ft (399m) but also passed through the High Hazel seam at a depth of 987ft (296m). In 1939, mining commenced in the Low Main seam at a depth of 2208ft (662m). As the deeper seams were worked out output increased at the High Hazel seam which was worked in three main districts: the North-West, South-East and South-West. Coal from all three districts was carried to the pit bottom by conveyor belts to be wound up to the surface. Coal mining and winding were carried out on the morning and afternoon shifts, with repair and maintenance work being undertaken at night. It was in the South-West district that the disaster occurred.

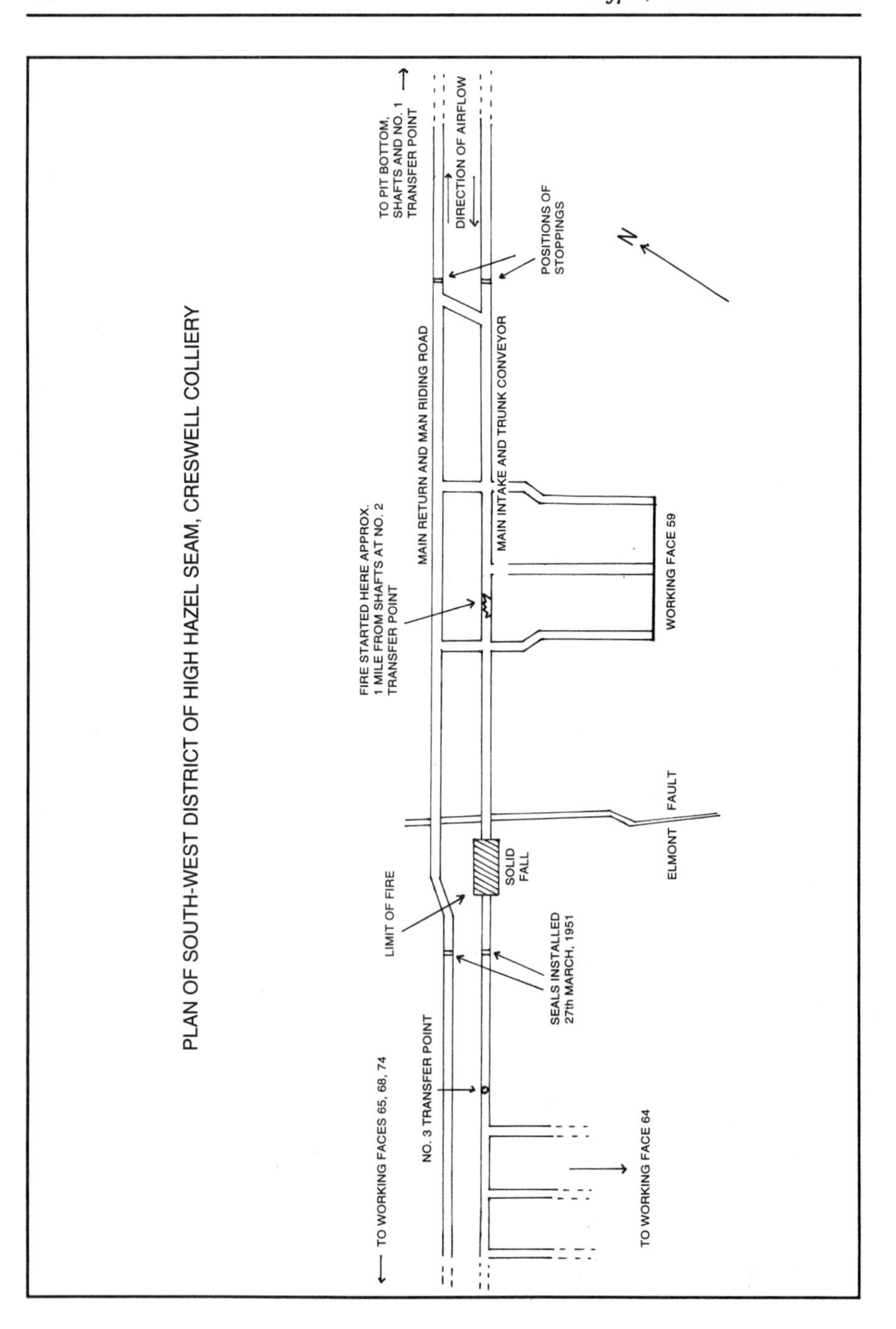
PLAN OF SOUTH-WEST DISTRICT OF HIGH HAZEL SEAM, CRESWELL COLLIERY
TO PIT BOTTOM, SHAFTS AND NO. 1 TRANSFER POINT
DIRECTION OF AIRFLOW
POSITIONS OF STOPPINGS
N
MAIN RETURN AND MAIN RIDING ROAD
MAIN INTAKE AND TRUNK CONVEYOR
FIRE STARTED HERE APPROX. 1 MILE FROM SHAFTS AT NO. 2 TRANSFER POINT
WORKING FACE 59
ELMONT FAULT
SOLID FALL
LIMIT OF FIRE
SEALS INSTALLED 27th MARCH, 1951
NO. 3 TRANSFER POINT
TO WORKING FACES 65, 68, 74
TO WORKING FACE 64

There were two main tunnels, or roads, serving the South-West district: the Main Intake, which was used for the transport of coal on conveyor belts and the Main Return along which ran two trains on an endless rope, and which carried men to and from the coal faces. This underground railway was referred to by the miners as 'the paddy.' Air was circulated through the tunnels by means of fans, entering via the Main Intake and leaving via the Main Return.

Coal was worked at five faces designated with the numbers 59, 64, 65, 68 and 74. The main conveyor system consisted of three belts working in tandem. No. 1 belt ran from the pit bottom to no. 2 transfer point, a distance of 1703yds (1.5km). No. 2 belt ran from here to no. 3 transfer point, a distance of 1080yds (972m) and no. 3 belt for a distance of 1060yds (954m) to the furthest coal face, no. 74. The coal from four of the five faces was delivered to no. 3 belt, the exception being face 59, the nearest to the pit bottom, whose coal went direct to no. 1 belt.

The fire began in the early hours of Tuesday, 26th September 1950. During the morning shift of the previous day it was noticed that the no. 2 conveyor belt was scored and at the beginning of the afternoon shift that day J.R. Hindley, a belt maintenance man, was called to examine it.

He discovered a groove which penetrated the belt for about two-thirds of its thickness and extended for a distance of about 300yds (270m). Hindley allowed the belt to be operated but inspected it at intervals and arrangements were made for him to repair the belt on overtime. These were cancelled, however, by H. Godfrey, the overman in charge of the night shifts who found that a large quantity of coal from no. 65 face had not been cleared and ordered that the belt be kept running. When Joshua Morris, the no. 3 transfer point attendant, arrived at work for the night shift at 11.00 p.m. on the 25th, he examined the no. 2 belt and found that for a distance of 6 to 8yds (5.5 to 7.25m) the groove had gone right through, becoming a slit through which he could put his hand. The damage had clearly worsened since Hindley's inspection but the belt was allowed to operate, nothing untoward being observed until 3.10 a.m. on the 26th when Morris signalled to William Hird, the attendant at the telephone 70yds (64m) to the east of no. 2 transfer point, to stop the belt. Morris had noticed a trailing piece of belt beneath the conveyor and told Hird over the telephone 'This belt is ripped down here. I want you to come down and see the extent of it'. Morris then began walking eastwards towards no. 2 transfer point which was about 1,000yds (900m) away, noting that a 400yds (360m) length of the bottom belt was ripped and some 40yds to 50yds (36m to 45m) of the top belt. 'I smelt some smoke then' he said later 'but I put it down to the pull on the haulage rope pulley'. As he continued walking, though, the smoke became more intense and when he was about 150yds (135m) from no. 2 transfer point he saw a red glow. As he drew closer, he saw a fire at the transfer chute and flames between the chute and the side wall of the tunnel.

Hird, meanwhile, after speaking to Morris on the telephone, had walked eastwards to the no. 2 transfer point where he saw the hopper full of pieces of torn conveyor belt. He returned to his post, telephoned F.W. Kirk who was manning the telephone exchange at the pit bottom and asked for the no. 1 belt to be stopped, but it continued to run. A few minutes later Hird saw fire in the chute at the transfer point and again telephoned Kirk, asking for the power to be cut off and help to be summoned. He had just completed the call when Morris arrived and asked him if he knew about the fire to which Hird replied that he had reported it. The time was now 3.45 a.m. Morris tried to tackle the fire with two portable fire extinguishers but the first had little effect and the second failed to function. Hird had not tried to extinguish the fire as he had previously been injured in a mining accident and was incapable of lifting an extinguisher.

The power, meanwhile, had been cut off and this brought John Rodda, overman in the North-West district, to the telephone to ask what was wrong. Kirk told him of the fire and asked him to come as quickly as possible. He then telephoned the manager and under manager at their homes and the Central Rescue Brigades at Chesterfield; officials from the N.C.B., the N.U.M. and H.M. Inspector of Mines were also summoned. When the under-manager, George Payton, arrived at the pit he immediately went underground and travelled to the scene of the fire having been assured that the men at the coal face had been warned and were on their way out. He found several members of the pit fire-fighting team led by Rodda, attempting to extinguish the fire. They had brought fire hoses but when they connected them to the water main it was found that the water pressure was totally inadequate. Their efforts with the hoses were later described as 'like standing in a garden watering flowers.'

It transpired that, in one of several mishaps which dogged the night's activities, the pump maintaining water pressure in the main had broken down. The men managed to obtain more portable fire extinguishers and supplies of sand and stone dust, which were used very effectively, and it was thought that they had the fire under control. Sadly this was far from the case, the steam and smoke having hidden the spread of the fire inwards along the roadway.

At 5.20 a.m. a team of fire-fighters arrived from Chesterfield Rescue Station but their efforts were severely hampered by the inadequate water supply. They donned breathing apparatus and attempted to get through and past the fire but the heat was too intense and the attempt failed. Eventually the water supply was restored, but by this time the fire had spread even further inwards. The water was now used to cool down the walls of the tunnel, and the fire-fighters again tried to advance down the roadway, but the walls and roof of the tunnel were now in a dangerously unstable condition and the men had to turn back.

Meanwhile, what of the men who had been trapped on the other side of the fire? Just after 4.00 a.m., Kirk had spoken to the manager or under manager – he could not remember which – and had been told to get the miners to the Main Return. He tried for twenty minutes to reach overman Godfrey on the telephone to pass on the message, but when he finally got through, the latter exclaimed 'Good God!' and dropped the receiver. That was the last that was heard from him so Kirk was unable to pass on the vital message to get the men out. He made several other calls, apparently, but the smoke soon drove him from his post and afterwards he could remember little of them. Tragically, whatever messages did get through to the coal faces, the miners did not seem to realise the seriousness of the situation. Some of them spent time hiding their tools, while others tried to carry them out. Some apparently sauntered from the coal faces, while others waited for 'the paddy' to come and take them out, their bodies later being found on the train. For many, the first sign of danger came when they walked into thick smoke and all they could do then was to try to dash through it to safety. Some made it, others didn't. One survivor was George Vardy of Creswell, working at 59 face, who later reported:

'I was working in the section with about 25 others when I thought I smelt something burning. I told Bill Morris, our deputy, and he went to investigate, but he did not get very far before he returned yelling "Clear the section!". Every one of us then made a belt for the pit shaft. The smoke was thick and it was getting very hot and I had to hold my breath as long as I could before I reached safety. I don't know how many of those who were working with me got out.'

Bill Morris was one of the few men who immediately realised the seriousness of the situation. He hurriedly collected his men together and led them to 59's left airway, in this way saving the lives of some thirty miners.

Men struggled to safety as the fire-fighters were attempting to extinguish the blaze, but it was soon realised that they were not coming out in the numbers expected. Rescue teams were sent in to explore the Main Return and almost immediately they found a body which they brought out. Shortly after, they brought out two more bodies and reported that they had seen ten more. The official report later commented:

'By this time the smoke in the Main Return at 59's left side return gate was extremely dense and had a very bad effect upon the eyes of the rescue men. Moreover, the effect of the smoke-laden air on the canary carried by the rescue teams showed that the atmosphere was so deadly that it was impossible to conceive of anyone being alive in the inbye workings. It was decided that, except for an exploration of the Main Return towards the shaft, rescue work should be stopped for the time being.'

Only a few hours after the fire broke out it was announced to the waiting pit-head crowd that there was now no hope for the eighty men trapped beyond the flames. The news was devastating, for few had realised the extent of the tragedy, events having occurred with such speed. The news was at first greeted with stunned silence, soon broken by sobbing and cries of grief.

Sealing the Site

A conference of the N.C.B. representatives, union officials and the Inspectorate was called and came to the conclusion that the only way to extinguish the fire, and to prevent an explosion of fire-damp (methane) was to seal the fire at selected sites. It was found, meanwhile, that the smoke had cleared somewhat from the Main Return, allowing the rescue teams to recover the ten bodies that they had seen and a further forty-seven which were a short distance further in. Twenty-seven more bodies were located but could not yet be recovered, and six men were still unaccounted for. Further in, the fire was still burning fiercely emphasising the need to build the seals as quickly as possible.

On the evening of the 6th September, while the rescue teams were engaged below in the grim task of recovering the bodies, a pit-head service was held at the colliery, conducted by the vicar of Creswell, the Reverend C.S. Branson, and attended by over a thousand people. Clergy from the neighbouring towns of Worksop, Clowne and Bolsover were present with several officials of the N.C.B. and N.U.M. A message of sympathy from King George V was read out; the king had written:

'We have heard of the disaster at Creswell Colliery with deep distress, and we send our heartfelt sympathy to the wives and families of those who have lost their lives.'

A message from the Prime Minister, Clement Attlee, was also read:

'I have heard with deep regret of the tragic loss of at least eighty men as the result of the fire at Creswell Colliery. Will you please convey our heartfelt sympathy to their families.' A bitterly cold wind blew as the crowd sang hymns under the grey evening sky, the service accompanied by the rattling of coal trains and the sound of bells from the pit-head gear.

Sites chosen for the two seals, one across the Main Return, the other across the Main Intake, were about 1,000yds (900m) from the pit bottom. The seals were built with sand-bags, the intake seal being 8yds (7.25m) long and the return seal 3ft (1m) shorter. The latter was particularly difficult to construct, the smoke in the tunnel forcing the men to wear breathing apparatus. Two teams worked in the return tunnel, each for two hour shifts, the work being arranged so that one team was relieved every hour. The fresh incoming group carried the sand-bags to the site while the team previously transporting material for an hour spent the second hour constructing the stopping. Each stopping was fitted with a 2 inches (5 cm) diameter steel tube so that samples of the atmosphere could be taken. When the seals were complete the teams withdrew from the mine, returning two days later to inspect them and strengthen them with 3ft (1m) brick walls.

The atmosphere behind the stoppings was sampled continuously by means of the steel tubes till it was established that the fire within the sealed-off area was completely extinguished. A meeting was held on 18th December 1950, when it was decided to re-open the workings at Easter, 1951. It was thought that this period would allow the rock strata to cool, and minimise the risk of the fire starting up again when air was allowed to reach the site of the combustion. The plan was duly put into operation, temporary stoppings having to be erected at intervals in the tunnels so that poisonous and inflammable gases, including large quantities of methane, could be safely removed in stages. The flow of air into the workings was also carefully controlled. All went according to plan until the tunnels were cleared as far as the Elmton Fault, where it was discovered that the air supply was severely restricted by an extensive rock fall. Furthermore, there was, at this time, a sudden drop in atmospheric pressure which resulted in an outflowing of toxic gases from within the workings. It was decided, therefore, to re-seal this part of the district, but before this was done twenty-seven more bodies were recovered, and two more located. It was found that the fire had extended from no. 2. transfer point inwards for a distance of 1,830ft (558m). The position of the new seals allowed a full inspection of the fire area, and permitted the conveyor road to be cleared and repaired so that full ventilation was available for the final opening of the workings on 11th August 1951, when the remaining six bodies were found and removed. The official report commented:

'In all three operations, as in the earlier work, the rescue teams drawn from a wide area did a fine job, working with diligence and courage, and performing hard and hazardous tasks without any untoward incident. It is noteworthy that some teams travelled as much as 1,500yds away from the fresh air base, thus making a total journey of 3,000yds.'

The Inquiry

The inquiry into the accident was opened by the Chief Inspector of Mines, Sir Andrew Meikle Bryan, at the Miners' Institute, Creswell, on 17th October 1950. Two days later, after twenty-six witnesses had given evidence about conditions and events leading up to the sealing of the fire area, Sir Andrew adjourned the inquiry. It was not until after investigators were able to study the site of the fire that the second stage of the inquiry was opened, on 27th November 1951. Eight new witnesses were called and four who had given evidence earlier were re-examined. The inquiry concluded on the following day and Sir Andrew sent his report to the Minister of Fuel and Power on 24th April 1952. The main points of the inquiry can be summarised as follows:

The Cause of the Fire

It was thought initially that the fire might have been caused by a fault in the electrical or mechanical equipment in the pit but this was quickly ruled out after a thorough examination showed that both were in excellent condition. This left the probable cause of the fire as heat generated by friction at the no. 2 transfer point. When the apparatus was examined after the district was un-sealed it was found that, despite the heat of the fire, some torn pieces of the conveyor belt were still present, wedged between the edge of the chute plate and the delivery drum of no. 2 conveyor. It seemed likely that the friction had occurred between these pieces of jammed material and the moving belt. Using pieces of belt and part of the Creswell conveyor system, set up on the surface, tests were carried out to see if this was the case. In one instance, smouldering occurred within two minutes, and fire a minute later. Sir Andrew commented;

'As a result of these experiments, I have no hesitation in coming to the conclusion that the fire underground was started by frictional heating of torn belting jammed between the top of the sloping chute plate and the moving no. 2 belt as it passed round the delivery roller of the top of the chute at the no. 2 transfer point.'

From the calculated area of missing conveyor belt it was estimated that there must have been some 1,600 lbs of torn belt (726kg) in the no. 2 chute at the time of the fire, and it seemed likely that this had been ignited by pieces of burning rubber falling on to it. A further experiment was carried out to establish how quickly the fire had taken hold in the chute, and how dense were the fumes which were given off. In an underground gallery at the Safety in Mines Research Institute at Buxton, a two-thirds scale model of the Creswell chute was built and filled with a proportionate amount of torn belting of a similar age and type to that used at Creswell, this then being ignited with two ounces (57gms) of burning rubber belt. The results were startling, the experimenter, Mr.S. Jones, reporting:

'about five minutes from the stage where you can say "Well, the fire is going well and it is not likely to go out" you have the sides of the chute red hot, and you have flames coming out of the mouth 12ft long.'

A few minutes later the heat generated was so intense that the concrete roof of the tunnel was starting to disintegrate and the fire had to be put out. The fumes were extremely dense, though no experiments were undertaken to determine the level of their toxicity. Sir Andrew recommended that, when they were commercially available, fire-proof conveyor belts should be installed in all mines.

The Tearing of the Belt

Another, almost equally important question, of course, was how the belt had come to be torn in the first place. It was known that pieces of shale and ironstone were sometimes deposited on the conveyor belt with the coal, and it seemed possible that a sharp piece of one of these rocks could have caused the tear. Again using re-erected conveyor apparatus, sharp pieces of shale were held against the moving belt. They cut into the belt to a limited extent but soon splintered, and it seemed unlikely that they had caused the damage. When a piece of iron-stone was used, however, it caused a deep cut in the belt 200yds long (180m), the amount of belt available for the experiment. It was concluded that a piece of ironstone had settled at the top of no. 2 chute – probably because of a build up of stone caused by no. 2 belt being operated while no. 1 was stationary – and that this had become wedged against the moving conveyor. At first it caused grooving in the belt and then cut right through it.

Of course, the damage to the belt had been spotted on the afternoon shift and arrangements made for it to be repaired, but tragically H. Godfrey, the night overman (who died of carbon monoxide poisoning) cancelled these arrangements. He may have thought, understandably, that as the belt had run safely on the afternoon shift it could continue to be used, but the fact remains that had the belt been repaired, the disaster would have been averted. Sir Andrew pointed out that it could also have been prevented if there had been a full-time attendant at no. 2 transfer point or if the conveyor had been fitted with a safety device of the Crosland type, which consisted of a hinged plate fitted at the top end of the chute and held by springs. Under an abnormal load the springs extended and cut off the electricity driving the conveyor.

The Failure of the Paddy

It was very unfortunate that at the time of the fire, just when men needed to get out in a hurry, the underground train, 'the paddy' was not running normally, due to work being carried out on the roadway. A few days before the disaster, work had begun to extend the run of the paddy from its terminus at the Elmton Fault to 74 coal face, giving a total distance of $2^1/_4$ml (3.5km). One of the trains was detached, and a pony employed to help with transportation. The actual sequence of events involving the paddy at the time of the fire, after its final routine trip bringing out face workers who had completed their night's work, is not clear. There were several telephone calls from the trapped men, the first at about 4.30 a.m. asking for the paddy to be sent in. The last call was from Leslie Hancock at the Elmton Fault who cried out to the haulage engineer, Frederick Hicks 'This is Leslie Hancock, this is Leslie Hancock, where is the train, where is the train? We are all about done here.' Attempts were made to send the train back in but these were thwarted by repeated and unexplained power failures. Finally the train reached the Elmton Fault but by then it was too late. No further messages were received from the trapped men, and the fumes finally drove Hicks from his post, making it impossible for the train to be operated. Sir Andrew commented:

'That the paddy could run only under the restrictions imposed by the repair work in progress at the time was bad enough, but that its movements were hampered by the presence of a pony or ponies and by the intermittent failure of the electric power and signalling systems by which not less than 30 valuable minutes were lost – was a double misfortune.'

Had the train been running normally when the first telephone call for it to be sent was received more lives could, probably, have been saved. The report recommended that repairs to man-riding trains should not be carried out when full shifts of men were at the faces, and that more attention should be paid to the ventilation of engine-houses.

The Provision of Intake Airways

Creswell Colliery's south-west district was ventilated by fans, the air entering by the Main Intake and leaving by the Main Return and travelling at a speed of about 500ft (150m) per minute. This is faster than a man could walk on the surface. Thus, when the fire broke out the fumes travelled rapidly inwards, towards the faces, and then outwards along the Main Return, overtaking men desperately trying to reach safety, and asphyxiating them. At one point the fleeing miners had to climb for 250yds (225m) up a 1 in 6 incline, and this is where many perished, the slope being referred to by Mr Sam Watson of the N.U.M. as 'the hill of death.' If the district had been equipped with two intake airways, the danger would have been greatly reduced: first, the velocity of air on the conveyor road would have been much lower and the fire would not have been fanned so vigorously; secondly, the speed of the fumes travelling inward would have been reduced, allowing more time to warn the men and for them to escape, and, thirdly, two intakes could be supplied with connecting passages, allowing fire-fighters to get ahead of the fire and halt its spread. Sir Andrew recommended that, wherever possible, mines should be supplied with two intake airways.

Immediate reactions to the Emergency

The enquiry highlighted the confusion, break-down in communications, and lack of urgency which followed the discovery of the fire, Sir Andrew stating:

'In the early messages sent in it does appear that no emphasis was laid on the need for all men in the district to leave their place of work immediately and hurry out by the return with all possible speed. This lack of emphasis no doubt arose from lack of precise knowledge of the nature of the fire, and the knowledge that good fire-fighting facilities were believed to exist.'

He added that it was difficult to avoid the feeling that too much attention was paid to fighting the fire, rather than ensuring the safety of the men.

Communications were hampered by the fact that the telephones were sometimes a considerable distance from the coal faces, in the case of 74's face, 430yds (387m) – almost a quarter of a mile. Furthermore, it seems that no general message urging immediate evacuation of the district was ever sent. The report recommended that telephones should be situated as close to the coal faces as possible and that there should be a distinctive general alarm signal, perhaps of the type produced by a klaxon.

Fire-fighting arrangements

The failure of the water supply at a critical time, indeed the only time it had been required to deal with a fire, was disastrous. Joshua Morris, when questioned about this at the enquiry, went so far as to say 'I honestly believe I could have coped with the fire. If the water supply had been adequate and a hose available I could have killed that fire.' The report recommended that the water pressure in the main at conveyor transfer points should be checked at the beginning of every shift, and that belts should not even be allowed to run if pressure was inadequate. Sir Andrew also suggested that fire-fighting procedures at every pit should be thoroughly checked and improved where necessary and that men stationed at transfer points should be well-trained in fire-fighting techniques and physically able to handle the equipment. (It will be remembered that William Hird was on light duties at the time due to a previous mine accident and was unable to carry a fire extinguisher).

The foregoing are the main features discussed in Sir Andrew Bryan's report. This concludes with a tribute to the heroism of many men, known and unknown, among the workmen, officials, management and rescue teams during the distressing hours immediately after the fire.

Despite advances in technology and safety procedures tragedies still occur underground. At the time of writing – August 1993 – three men have been killed at Bilsthorpe Colliery in Nottinghamshire. A section of roof collapsed 2,000ft (610m) below the surface, blocking the passage for a length of 160ft (48m). Three men were rescued, by men removing the rock by hand, working singly in twenty minute shifts in the confined space. Working underground will always be dangerous.

THE LONG TUNNELS

Clay Cross

The most spectacular examples of the work of the Victorian railway engineers are probably the great bridges such as those at Saltash, Clifton and the Firth of Forth. Less obvious are the long railway tunnels but they often required considerably more effort, ingenuity and dogged determination to build. Some of the longest railway tunnels in the British Isles are those which were excavated to carry the railways through the peaks of North Derbyshire.

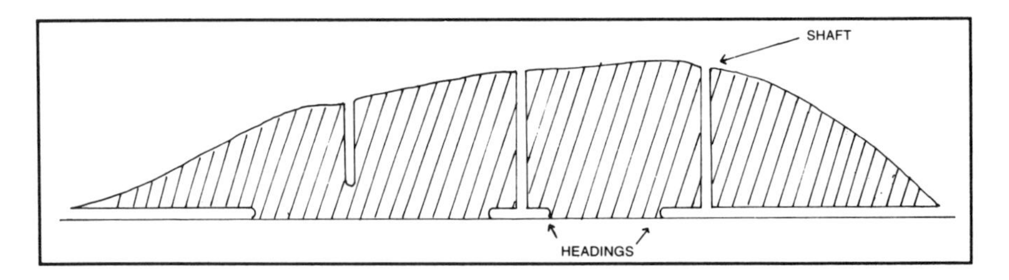

Plan showing method of excavating a tunnel

The first stage of tunnel construction was to survey the land and mark out the line of the tunnel, trial bores then being drilled to determine the nature of the rock to be excavated. Working shafts were then sunk to the level of the tunnel and, from the foot of each shaft, pilot tunnels, or 'headings' were excavated in each direction. Once the headings had met, the longitudinal line of the tunnel could be set out with greater accuracy, and drainage and ventilation improved. The tunnel could then be enlarged to its full bore and lined with bricks or stonework. Navvies were lowered to the bottom of the shafts in huge metal buckets, powered by horse-gins, the buckets also being used to remove spoil from the

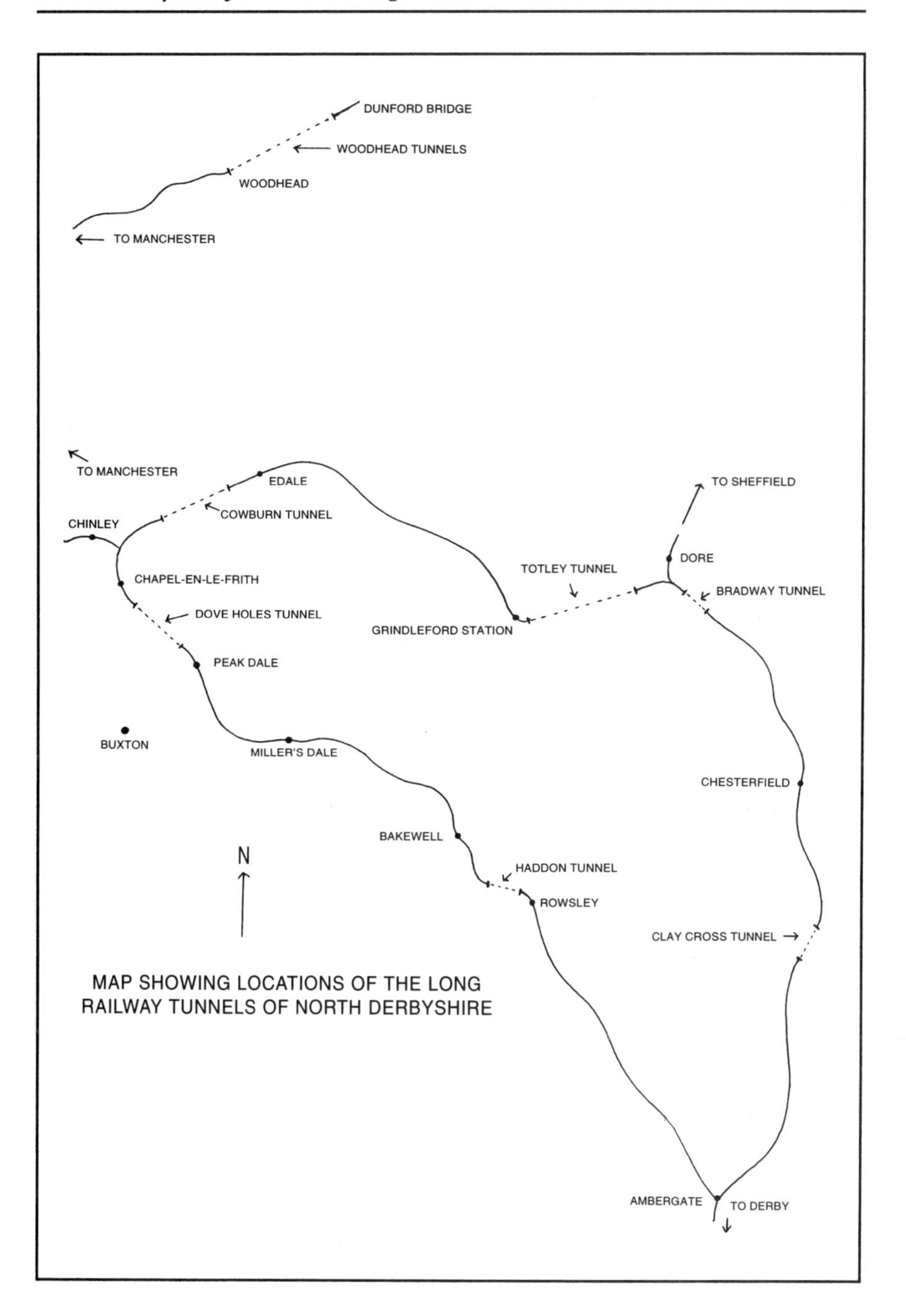

MAP SHOWING LOCATIONS OF THE LONG RAILWAY TUNNELS OF NORTH DERBYSHIRE

workings. Despite the advances in steam technology during the 19th century the great tunnels of the period were built largely by sheer manpower, the work being dirty, exhausting and dangerous.

The first half of the 19th century was the hey-day of the pioneering railway engineers, and this brief survey of Derbyshire's longest railway tunnels begins with the illustrious name of George Stephenson. In 1835 Stephenson surveyed the route for the North Midland Railway Company's line between Derby and Leeds, in his capacity of Engineer-in-Chief. Seven tunnels were needed, the longest of which was to be driven beneath the industrial town of Clay Cross, about 5ml (8km) south of Chesterfield.

Stephenson and his resident engineer, F. Swanwick, awarded the tunnel contract to Edward Price and work began in February 1837, the excavation proceeding from both tunnel entrances and from ten shafts. The bore was driven through shale and extensive seams of coal, so extensive that the shrewd Stephenson formed his own company to mine them, which, ten years later, became the Clay Cross Company.

By the end of 1838, 400yds (360m) of tunnel had been excavated, but work was increasingly delayed by vast quantities of water flowing from the saturated coal measures, this having to be continually pumped from the workings. Fifteen horse-gins were used to remove spoil from the tunnel and work continued round the clock, sightseers coming from far around to watch the navvies labouring in the glare of huge bonfires. Accidents were frequent and it is thought that eleven men were killed during construction.

The tunnel, 1 mile and 24yds long (1.6km) and lined throughout with red brick, was completed in 1840, its northern entrance being embellished with castellated towers in the style of a Moorish gateway: it is now a listed building. Early in the morning of 11th May that year, George Stephenson and his guest George Hudson, the Yorkshire railway tycoon, climbed aboard the inaugural train at Chesterfield to travel to Derby. The train was helped up the long incline to the Clay Cross tunnel by a pilot engine which left it at the north portal. However, when about three quarters of the distance through the tunnel, the engine stalled through lack of steam and a man had to be sent back to recall the pilot engine. The passengers, meanwhile, began to climb down from the carriages and wander about in the tunnel, until an exasperated Stephenson urged them to return to their places, his strong voice with its Northumbrian accent rising above the commotion. The pilot engine soon returned, though, and the train arrived at Derby at 9.30 a.m.

Dove Holes

Dove Holes Tunnel was bored through Cow Low in the Peaks between 1860 and 1863 to take the line from Derby to Manchester. Difficulties were met from the very outset, the main problem being the waterlogged, cavern-riddled nature of the terrain, as the Chief Engineer, William Henry Barlow, later described:

'Between what is now the south end of the tunnel and the turnpike road, there are some limestone quarries in the direct course of the railway, in the rocks of which are many natural fissures which form caverns of various depths. Shortly before commencing the works it was found that a considerable body of water was running through one of these fissures, the flow being distinctly audible in the quarry. Ladders, ropes and lights were obtained; the fissure was explored and at a depth of 30ft a very considerable stream of water was seen. The effect of this discovery led to such an impression of the peculiarity of the district, and the costly and speculative character of all works carried out on it, that contractors declined to undertake the responsibility except on terms which were considered excessively high. This was an unexpected difficulty to the Company but, after much deliberation, it was decided to make the tunnel without a contractor.'

The underground river was the continuation of a brook which ran from the Buxton area to Swallow Hole where it disappeared underground. The river had to be diverted away from the tunnel area, this being achieved by cutting a channel near the Swallow Hole, along which the stream could run in the direction of the Great Rocks Dale. However, as Mr Barlow recalled:

'Now another remarkable circumstance occurred. The river ran along its new course to a point about half a mile south of the tunnel; but here it found another fissure, into which it fell and disappeared. So matters continued for some six months, when, it seems, the brook filled this underground cistern; and then it resumed its course along the diverted watercourse which had been provided for it. The course cut for the brook is a total length of nearly two miles through land over which the company had no legal power; and so great was the difficulty, even under the special circumstances, of acquiring this right that eventually parliamentary authority had to be secured to take possession of the land.'

Southern entrance to Dove Holes Tunnel

Work now began on sinking the shafts and tunnelling inwards from the northern end of the tunnel, but progress was slow owing to the extreme hardness of the rocks and – despite the main watercourse having been diverted – the waterlogged nature of the terrain. Six steam engines, of from twenty to fifty horse-power, were constantly employed in draining the workings. When the tunnel was completed, a culvert, 3ft (approx. 1m), wide was dug between the two railway tracks and roofed with a semi-circular brick arch, the crown of which was about 12ins (approx. 0.3m) beneath the sleepers. The flow of water was sufficient to supply locomotive water columns at Chapel-en-le-Frith, Chinley and Gowhole sidings.

The Dove Holes Tunnel was completed in 1863 having been driven through a variety of strata including mountain limestone, old red sandstone and shale. It is 1ml 1,224yds (2.75km) long, lined throughout with brick and has eight shafts. The tracks in the tunnel descend from the south end towards Chapel-en-le-Frith at a rate of 1 in 90, the difference in level between the entrances being about 100ft (30m).

On June 19th, 1872 a section of the tunnel collapsed, a further fall occurring, nearly seventy years later, on February 2nd, 1940, following a night of torrential rain. On this occasion a south-bound train ploughed into the rubble, but further disaster was averted by the guard who picked his way through the tunnel to warn the driver of a north-bound train. The tunnel is now closed to passenger traffic but still used by goods trains.

Haddon

On 25th May 1860, the Act was passed which allowed the railway to be extended from Rowsley to Buxton. The 6th Duke of Devonshire, who owned Chatsworth Park and extensive lands to the north of Rowsley, had already given permission for the line to go through the Chatsworth estate, but by 1860 he was dead and his successor would not entertain the proposal. An alternative route had to be found, the only way possible being up the Wye Valley to Bakewell which meant going through the grounds of Haddon Hall, a mile (1.6km) to the north of Rowsley. The owner of Haddon, the Duke of Rutland, agreed to this providing that no trees were lopped or felled and that the line was concealed in a tunnel for its entire length through the park.

Work commenced in the cutting which led to the eastern entrance of the tunnel on 4th September 1860, keepers being posted to watch the grounds, to report any damage and to prevent the navvies stealing game. Much of the tunnel was constructed by the 'cut and cover' method, a deep cutting being covered with arched masonry and then with rock and soil. Five shafts were sunk, the deepest of which was only twelve ft (3.5m) the headings being joined on 11th March 1861. Four months later disaster struck when part of the tunnel collapsed, killing four men outright and seriously injuring a fifth who died the next day. The completed tunnel was 1,058yds (952m) long and is now disused, the line from Matlock to Peak Dale being closed in the 1960s.

Wreckage of collapsed Haddon Tunnel

Bradway

The hills to the north of Dronfield had long presented a formidable barrier to a direct rail-link between Sheffield and the southern part of the Midland Railway system, but between 1867 and 1870 the building of the

Bradway Tunnel, under the direction of engineer John Crossley made it possible to open the line from Chesterfield to Sheffield. Northbound trains enter the tunnel a mile (1.6km) from Dronfield after climbing a long gradient of 1 in 100. At the tunnel entrance the gradient reverses, falling at 1 in 100 to Sheffield. The shale and sandstone through which the tunnel was bored was saturated, as F.W. Williams wrote in his book *The Midland Railway* (1877):

'In sinking the shafts of this tunnel the influx of water was so great that it is estimated some 16,000 gallons flowed in every hour, and it had to be pumped out by means of seven or eight engines erected for this purpose, and working day and night.'

Some of this water was conveyed to Sheffield where it was used in supply tanks for locomotives. The completed tunnel had six shafts and was 1ml 267yds (1.87km) long, being lined throughout with brick and masonry.

Cowburn

The last of the trans-peak railway routes to be constructed was that between Dore in the east and Chinley in the west. At the western end of the line the Vale of Edale is linked with the valley of Black Brook by the Cowburn Tunnel which is 2ml 182yds long (3.3km). Work on the tunnel began in 1888, a major problem being the extremely hard nature of the rock – mainly millstone grit – which proved very resistant even to the improved drills and explosives which were by now available.

The bore passes directly under Cowburn, and the summit of the Dore and Chinley line is located in the tunnel, the line rising at 1 in 1,000 for 913yds (821m) from the eastern portal and then falling to Chinley at 1 in 150. The difference in height between the two entrances is 53ft (16m). There is only one permanent shaft to the tunnel, the excavation of which was an achievement in itself, for it is nearly 900ft (270m) deep, perhaps the deepest shaft on any British railway tunnel. The shaft is a few yards to the north of the tunnel, over a large circular chamber connected to the bore by a side opening. At one stage, water collected in the shaft to a depth of 90ft (27m), the men working in diving bells until the headings met and the water could be pumped out and taken to Chinley where it was used by locomotives.

On completion, in 1892, the tunnel was lined throughout, partially with stonework but mainly with brick, some twenty million bricks being used in the tunnel and shaft. The portals are of stonework and train passengers entering the eastern portal can see that the masonry has been reinforced with iron hoops.

Cowburn Tunnel entrance at Upper Booth

The shaft is surmounted up on the moor by a square, castellated stone tower, 20ft (6m) high and with sides 22ft (6.5m) long. This can be seen from many points including the main A625 Castleton road. Further surface evidence of the tunnel consists of an area of hummocky ground above the eastern entrance at Upper Booth. This is known as 'The Tips' and is spoil dumped during excavation of the tunnel. The area around Upper Booth and The Tips is said to be haunted by a phantom black dog, an archetypal apparition reported in many parts of the British Isles including, it will be recalled, the Derbyshire lead mines. In 1930 a lady called Greta Shirt saw the creature one evening near Upper Booth and, believing it to be an ordinary dog, went to stroke it. To her surprise she could not feel it and was even more shocked when it walked through a wire fence and disappeared.

Spoil from Cowburn Tunnel at The Tips

Totley

Totley Tunnel is situated at the eastern end of the Dore and Chinley rail route, part of it being in Derbyshire and part in west Yorkshire. The Derbyshire portal is in the Derwent Valley, 5ml (8km) north of Chatsworth and about 100yds (91m) from Grindleford Station. Waterlogged terrain, which had caused so many problems with the other Derbyshire tunnels, proved an almost insurmountable obstacle with the construction of the Totley Tunnel.

The resident engineer was Percy Richard and the contractor Thomas Oliver. Four permanent and three temporary shafts were sunk, all, due to difficulties with access and the height of Totley Moor – 1,300ft (390m) above sea-level – within three quarters of a mile (1.25km) from the Totley end. Pumps and air-lines were thus needed to ventilate the workings. Excavation of the first temporary shaft, at the mouth of the tunnel, was begun on 24th September 1888, water being struck after only 8ft (2.5m), a portent of things to come. By the time the shaft had reached its full depth, two months later, water was pouring from the saturated shale at the rate of 10,000 gallons per hour. The sinking of the other two temporary shafts was slightly easier as much of the water from the surrounding rocks had been removed through the first.

The permanent shafts were also begun in September. Numbered 1 to 4 from the Totley end, no. 1 was completed on October 30th and no. 2 on December 1st. Water was still a major problem, however, 8,000 gallons per hour pouring into no. 3 shaft which had to be temporarily abandoned. No. 4 shaft was begun on September 20th, but incessant flooding delayed its construction until June the following year, by which time 26,000 gallons of water were being pumped out every hour. A report of the time commented 'If the persons in charge had wished to tap every spring in the hill they could not have done so more successfully.'

Horizontal tunnelling had begun at the Grindleford entrance on 27th September 1888, but had to be halted from June to August the following year while a drain was built to carry away the water. At the Totley end, headings were being driven from the shafts, but work had to be frequently abandoned while water was pumped out. No headings could be driven from no. 3 shaft until the bore from no. 2 reached it and the water drained away. The bore reached no. 4 shaft on 21st September 1889, giving a continuous length from the Totley end of 1,167yds (1km). However, work was again halted, for six weeks, in the summer of 1890 while a dam was built across the tunnel to allow the building of a better drainage system, tunnelling recommencing on 11th August. At the Grindleford end the bore had reached a length of 1800yds (1.5km) when, on November 16th, a stream broke through the roof, requiring the construction of yet another drain. Work began again on 26th

Contractor's train at Totley Tunnel shortly before its opening in 1893

February 1892, and finally on 23rd October that year, the two headings met.

163 tons of gelignite were used during construction, spoil being hauled up no. 4 shaft, the deepest and widest of the shafts, and dumped around it, or carried out of the tunnel by a pony-drawn, narrow-gauge railway. The tunnel was lined throughout, mainly with brick, some thirty million bricks having been used. The tracks had been laid by 2nd September 1893, and the line was opened to goods traffic on 6th November that year. Passenger services began on 13th May 1894. A further ventilation shaft was sunk in that year, almost at the mid-point of the tunnel, this being 697ft (209m) deep and 20ft (6m) in diameter. Like the Cowburn Tunnel shaft this was set off-centre, descending into a chamber connecting to the main tunnel.

Trains entering the eastern entrance have to climb several steep gradients of up to 1 in 100 before reaching a short level section and the summit. The remaining 2,000yds (1.87km) fall at 1 in 1,000. The tunnel is not completely straight, the tracks entering the Derbyshire portal on a curve of half a mile radius. At 3ml 950yds (5.7km) it is, after the Severn Tunnel, the second longest rail tunnel in Britain and lengthmen's cabins are set into the sides.

Construction of the Dore to Chinley line with its two long tunnels, Cowburn and Totley, gave the Midland Railway direct access to Manchester from Sheffield. Formerly all traffic had to make a long circuitous journey by way of Chesterfield and Ambergate, joining the Derby to Manchester line via Matlock and Millers Dale.

Bolsover

Bolsover Tunnel was built in 1905 for the Lancashire, Derbyshire and East Coast Railway as part of a grand scheme to link the coal fields of Derbyshire and Nottinghamshire with both the Lancashire and East Coast Ports. The only part of the line to be completed, however, was that between Chesterfield and Lincoln, with a branch to Beighton. The tunnel was 1ml 865yds (2.4km) long and driven through limestone and shale. It had two shafts and was lined throughout with brick. Mining subsidence was a continual source of damage to the tunnel, this being one reason that the line between Chesterfield and Langwith Junction was closed in 1951.

Construction of Bolsover Tunnel

The Woodhead Tunnels

When the great engineer George Stephenson heard of the proposal to bore a three-mile tunnel (approx. 5km) through the southern Pennines between Woodhead and Dunford Bridge, to take the railway from Manchester to Sheffield, he laughed in disbelief and declared he would eat the first train to go through. Stephenson's scepticism was understandable – the proposed tunnel would be almost twice as long as Brunel's Box Tunnel near Bath, itself an incredible achievement – but he was mistaken. The Woodhead Tunnel was built but it took seven years' work, enormous expense, and the lives of over thirty men.

A tunnel had been suggested as early as 1831 but nothing was done until 1835 when the Sheffield, Ashton-under-Lyne and Manchester Railway Company was formed. Plans were commissioned from two eminent engineers, Charles Blacker Vignoles and Joseph Locke, and the line was authorised by an Act of Parliament in 1837. Initially Vignoles' plan, rather than Locke's, was approved and, on 1st October 1838, the chairman of the company, Lord Wharncliffe, ceremonially dug the first sod at Saltersbrook, a mile (approx. 1.6km) east of Woodhead and 1,500ft (450m) above sea level.

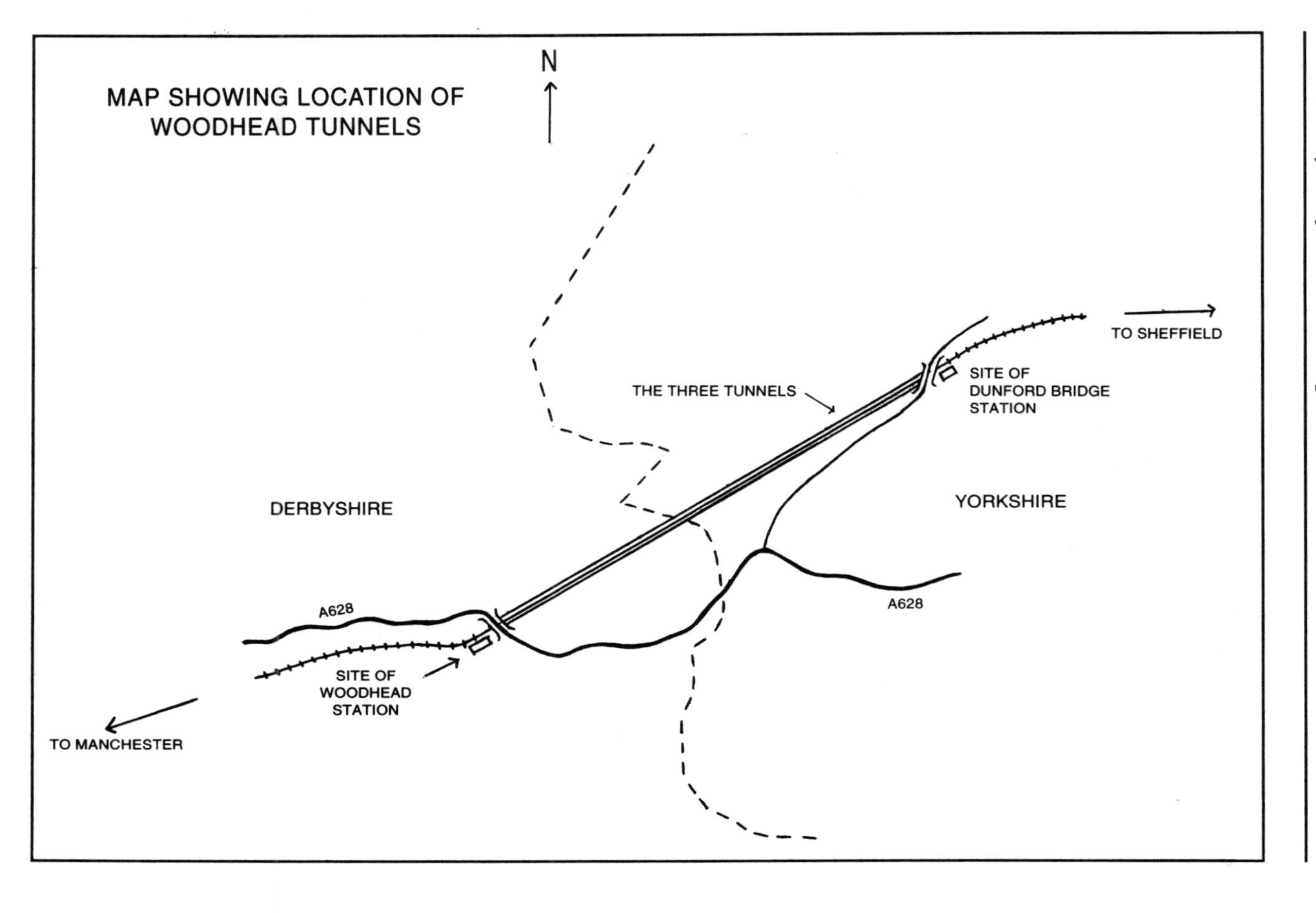
MAP SHOWING LOCATION OF
WOODHEAD TUNNELS
N
TO SHEFFIELD
SITE OF
DUNFORD BRIDGE
STATION
THE THREE TUNNELS
DERBYSHIRE
YORKSHIRE
A628
A628
SITE OF
WOODHEAD
STATION
TO MANCHESTER

Work was difficult from the outset: the nearest large town to Woodhead (then in Cheshire but now part of Derbyshire) was Glossop, about 9ml (14km) away, and simply transporting materials and provisions from there to the workings was a major undertaking. Rain was continual and exacerbated the already difficult task of working on the steep hillsides above Woodhead.

Five shafts, each 10ft (3m) in diameter, were sunk from the moor down to tunnel level, and the navvies then began tunnelling outwards, one gang to the west and one to the east, at the foot of each shaft. Tunnelling also began at the Woodhead and Dunford Bridge entrances. Twelve rock faces could therefore be worked at once.

The navvies lived in appalling conditions on the moors, some in tents and stone shelters, provided by the company, others in huts made of mud, stone and turf that they built themselves. Working conditions were equally bad. Water poured continually from the rocks into the shafts and tunnel, the men working knee-deep in mud and soaked to the skin. The water was a particular problem in no. 2 shaft where at one stage 100,000 gallons per day were being pumped out. It was estimated that eight million tons of water were pumped from the tunnel during construction.

Financial problems dogged the project, and both Lord Wharncliffe and Charles Vignoles were forced to resign in a dispute over shares. The latter, who had apparently been unpopular with the directors of the company, was sued by them after his departure, and lost about £80,000. Vignoles was replaced in 1840 by Joseph Locke who, it seems, had been retained by the company as a consultant, though Locke broadly followed his predecessor's plan. As the tunnelling grew ever more difficult the costs rose sharply. By 1842 the original estimate of the tunnel's cost had risen from £60,000 to £200,000. Sometimes, the money ran out and work came to a complete halt while more funds were raised.

Below ground, meanwhile, the navvies hacked, blasted and shovelled their way through millstone grit, shales, sandstone, slate and clay. The navvies, of course, were a breed apart, being labourers of a particularly specialised nature. In the past they had built roads, sea-walls and canals, but as the 19th century progressed they were increasingly employed on the ever expanding network of railways. It took a year's hard work to turn a strong man into a navvy. A typical day's work for such a man would be to lift twenty tons of earth or rock with a shovel, over his head, into a railway wagon. They had phenomenal appetites, phenomenal thirsts and were often uncontrollable, particularly when drunk, though they could be fiercely loyal to a good employer. They usually lived in huge camps, moving from one great work to another and being seldom seen in towns. They were well-paid by the standards of the time, though often forced to pay excessive prices for food and other provisions at shops owned by the contractors. Navvies often sustained appalling injuries and, due to bad living and working conditions, suffered all manner of diseases and complaints. At Woodhead they were treated by Henry Pomfret, a surgeon from Hollingworth, 8ml (13km) away, who was employed not by the company but by the navvies themselves, who paid a voluntary contribution each week. He was popular among the men, calling regularly to the tunnel three times a week, and going out any time of the day or night in emergencies, often in atrocious weather – the outward journey often took him two hours.

In July 1845, Pomfret listed the injuries he had encountered, the list including 23 cases of compound fracture, among them two fractured skulls; 74 simple fractures and 140 serious cases of burns, contusions, lacerations and dislocations: 32 men had been killed, he reported, and several more severely maimed. In addition there had been 400 cases of relatively minor injuries involving lacerations, bruisings, broken shins and broken fingers (seven of which were amputated). This was not even a complete list, for the men at the eastern end of the tunnel had, for two years, been treated by a different surgeon. Edwin Chadwick, the great social reformer, pointed out that the casualties at the Woodhead Tunnel were on a par with those that could be expected at a major battle such as that of Waterloo.

Many people in authority blamed the accidents on the men themselves, not entirely without reason for the navvies were habitually reckless and frequently drunk – Pomfret said that many men often set out to work in a state of intoxication. However, many deaths were due to a complete lack of concern for safety procedures by those in charge and the policy of keeping costs down at the expense of safety. A common cause of death and injury, for example, was the use of iron stemmers in blasting. A stemmer was a rod used to pack gunpowder, and then a clay filling, into a hole drilled in the rock, before blasting and if the stemmer scraped the rock it could cause sparks which prematurely ignited the gunpowder. Copper stemmers would have been much safer as the metal was softer and less likely to spark but Wellington Purdon, assistant engineer, rejected their use because copper was too expensive. Consequently men continued to be maimed and killed, as was described before a House of Commons Select Committee investigating working conditions on the railways:

'William Jackson, miner, no. 5 shaft. He was looking over John Webb's shoulder, while he was stemming a hole charged with powder, when the blast went off, blowing the stemmer through Jackson's head and killed him on the spot.'

Purdon was also criticised for not using safety fuses for blasting, again on the grounds of time and expense.

The navvies also contributed each week into a sick fund to provide eight shillings a week to a man who was injured or ill and if a navvy was killed it was the custom for each man to pay a shilling to cover the expenses of the funeral and to donate something to his widow. Generally a navvy's funeral was an impressive affair and people were often surprised at the dignified behaviour of the mourners, men who were normally so wild and reckless. Those killed at the Woodhead Tunnel were buried at Woodhead Chapel and at Penistone Parish Church. The graves are unmarked, the only record of the deaths being in the parish register and sometimes their names were not even known.

Despite the deaths and injuries, the accidents and the financial set-backs, the work went on and finally, in the winter of 1845, the tunnel was completed. On December 20th the Board of Trade Inspector, General Paisley, rode through the tunnel and declared that it was the best he had ever seen. At ten o'clock on Tuesday 23rd December, a train of twenty carriages left the Sheffield Terminus pulled by two engines, carrying company directors, engineers, local gentry and the shareholders. It stopped at Dunford Bridge for twenty minutes, to take on water and then passed through the tunnel, arriving ten minutes later at Woodhead.

Excavation of the second Woodhead Tunnel began in 1847 and was less expensive and less dangerous than that of the first. The geological conditions were now familiar and no new surface shafts were necessary as the engineers, realising that a second tunnel would later be needed, had driven twenty-five arches at 200yds (180m) intervals into the north wall of the first bore, and excavations could now proceed from these. Working conditions were better and the number of deaths and injuries was greatly reduced, but in 1849 cholera, then widespread in England, struck at Woodhead. There was no vaccine and twenty-eight men died, in addition to two local women who had come to nurse them. Many workmen, and some villagers, deserted the site when they saw many coffins being brought up to Woodhead. Eventually, however, the outbreak subsided, the men returned and work continued, the tunnel being finally completed in 1852. Both tunnels were just over 3ml (approx. 5km) long.

The tunnels seem to have had an evil reputation in the area for a long time after. Fatal accidents and cholera, which some local people called 'the plague', were not forgotten and conditions for train drivers and maintenance men were appalling. It was pitch-black in the tunnels, the air foul and stinking. The only lights visible on an engine's footplate were the fire and the gauge lamp, the latter sometimes going out through lack of oxygen. Heavy coal trains could take over half an hour to pass through the tunnels, the drivers being forced to breathe through damp rags to filter out carbon dioxide and sulphurous fumes. The tunnels were bottle-necks on a line which for much of its length had quadruple tracks and, in an attempt to keep traffic running quickly through them, a signal box was installed inside the second or 'up' tunnel. However, crews could not be found to man it, even for a reduced shift of six hours, and the idea was abandoned. It was the gangers who fared the worst, though. They could barely see to work, even with the aid of powerful lamps and some men were disabled by pneumono-silicosis after only six years in the damp, smoky conditions. The two Woodhead tunnels had been in use for some ninety years when, in 1936, the L.N.E.R. decided to electrify the line between Sheffield Victoria and Manchester London Road (now Piccadilly). Work was apparently well underway when war broke out and the project was halted. After the war it was decided that it would be too costly to install electric cables in the Woodhead tunnels which in any case were becoming difficult and expensive to maintain. The decision was taken, therefore, to build a new twin-track bore parallel to the old tunnels. Balfour Beatty & Co. Ltd. were awarded the contract, the project being directed by John Isdale Campbell, Chief Civil Engineer of B.R.'s Eastern Region. The resident engineer was J.D.Dempster.

Work commenced in February 1949, with the sinking of a 16ft (5m) shaft from the moors to the tunnel level 467ft (approx. 140m) below, and by 16th May 1951, a 12-feet (approx. 3.5m) square pilot tunnel had been completed. Work now began on enlarging the tunnel to a diameter of 30ft (9m) but progress was halted when the excavation ran into water-bearing shale, some 900ft (270m) from the Woodhead entrance. Attempts were made to brace the unstable rock with strong steel ribs but after a few days these began to buckle. Further strengthening was undertaken but again, after a few days, the steel-work began to give way. It was considered too dangerous to continue working in the area so men and equipment were withdrawn, narrowly averting a tragedy for – only a few hours later – the roof of the tunnel collapsed, bringing down tons of rock and twisted steel and leaving a gaping void above.

Drastic measures were obviously called for, the first step in repairing the damage being the construction of a massive concrete bulkhead across the tunnel, as close to the fallen section as was possible. With the weakened roof supported, work began on clearing the fallen rock, this being brought out through an opening in the bulkhead. As the tunnel was cleared, steel ribs conforming to the shape of the finished tunnel were erected at 12 inch (30cm) intervals. Longitudinal framework was then added and concrete piped behind, forming an arched lining 3ft (approx. 1m) thick. When the debris had been entirely cleared, an extra layer of concrete was added, making this 100ft (30m) long section 5ft (1.5m) thick. The bulkhead was then removed.

It took six months to clear the debris from the rock fall and so that work could proceed on other parts of the excavation a by-pass tunnel was constructed. This simplified the removal of spoil, which had been a problem from the outset of tunnelling and allowed work to proceed on nine enlargement faces. Half a million cubic yards (380,000 cu.m) of rock were removed and, as with the earlier tunnels, water had to be pumped continually out of the workings.

The railway track was laid by the end of 1953 and the tunnel opened to traffic on June 3rd, 1954. It was 3ml 66yds (approx. 5km) long, cost £4.25 million and despite the advances over the years in safety precautions, equipment and working conditions, six men were killed. Were the loss of life and the expense worthwhile? The new Woodhead Tunnel is no longer in use, the line having been closed in 1981, and its entrance is sealed with a metal grill.

The two old tunnels remained derelict until the 1960s, when it was decided by the Central Electricity Generating Board to use the second tunnel to carry high voltage cables. The original plan had been to use pylons but there was a strong protest from the Peak Park Planning Board and other groups who did not want to see the moors defaced. The old tunnel provided an excellent alternative, though extensive renovation was needed. One problem was the thick accumulation of soot, but this could not be washed off as the resulting dirty water would have drained into the River Etherow which fed Manchester's reservoirs. The solution was to use high-pressure air jets to blow off the soot, though it was a dirty and laborious job for the men concerned. When the soot had settled it was neutralised with lime and mixed with cement into the old railway ballast to form a hard floor. The walls needed repair work, having been distorted by water pressure behind them over the years, and the pointing being destroyed by water and corrosive fumes. Along one side of the new floor the power cables were laid in a double concrete trough which is water cooled, there being weirs at intervals to cope with the 85ft (26m) fall from one end of the tunnel to the other. Cable joints on top of the trough are cooled by electric fans at the tunnel entrances. A narrow-gauge railway now carries maintenance vehicles in and out.

It is possible to walk or drive down to the tunnel mouths by turning off the main A628 road on to a narrow, bumpy track, though the old tunnel entrances are fenced off and partially obscured by Electricity Board huts. It is hard to imagine the bustle of activity as the tunnels were built, or the clatter as the trains rushed through. Woodhead Station has long gone, as have the tracks, only the deserted platforms remaining. On a cold, grey day it seems the loneliest place in the world.

Entrances to the three Woodhead tunnels. The two old tunnels are on the left

NOTTINGHAM SUBTERRANEA

The City of Caves

At least 400 caves are known to exist beneath the city of Nottingham, all these having been cut by man out of the soft, easily worked, sandstone. The caves are of two basic types: those dug out of exposed rock faces, often used as dwellings, and those excavated beneath the surface of the ground, used as cellars, store-rooms, etc.

It is not known precisely when the first of Nottingham's caves were excavated. In Victorian times, and even later, there were theories of vast troglodyte settlements of great antiquity, but such ideas are now discounted, there is no evidence whatever to support the stories. Probably the earliest reference to caves in Nottingham is that by Archbishop Asser, the 10th century chronicler, in his book *The Life of King Alfred.* Discussing the invasion of the Danes in 868, he writes:

'In the same year the above-named army of Pagans, leaving Northumberland, invaded Mercia, and advanced to Nottingham, which is called in the British tongue *Tigguacobanc,* but in the Latin, *Speluncarum Domum,* the place or house of caves, and they wintered there that same year.'

It is probable that some caves were excavated by the Celts and Saxons but the earliest that can be dated with any certainty are of the 12th and 13th centuries.

By the 14th century there were many cave dwellings in Nottingham, these often being referred to in Borough records. In 1300, for example, there is reference to 'a messuage [dwelling] that lies in the rock at the Milne Holes and it extends towards the mills of the Lord King's Castle'. This probably was one of the caves on Gilly Flower Hill which was destroyed during the building of the People's College in the 1960s. In 1316 there is reference to cellars beneath the Saturday Market at Long

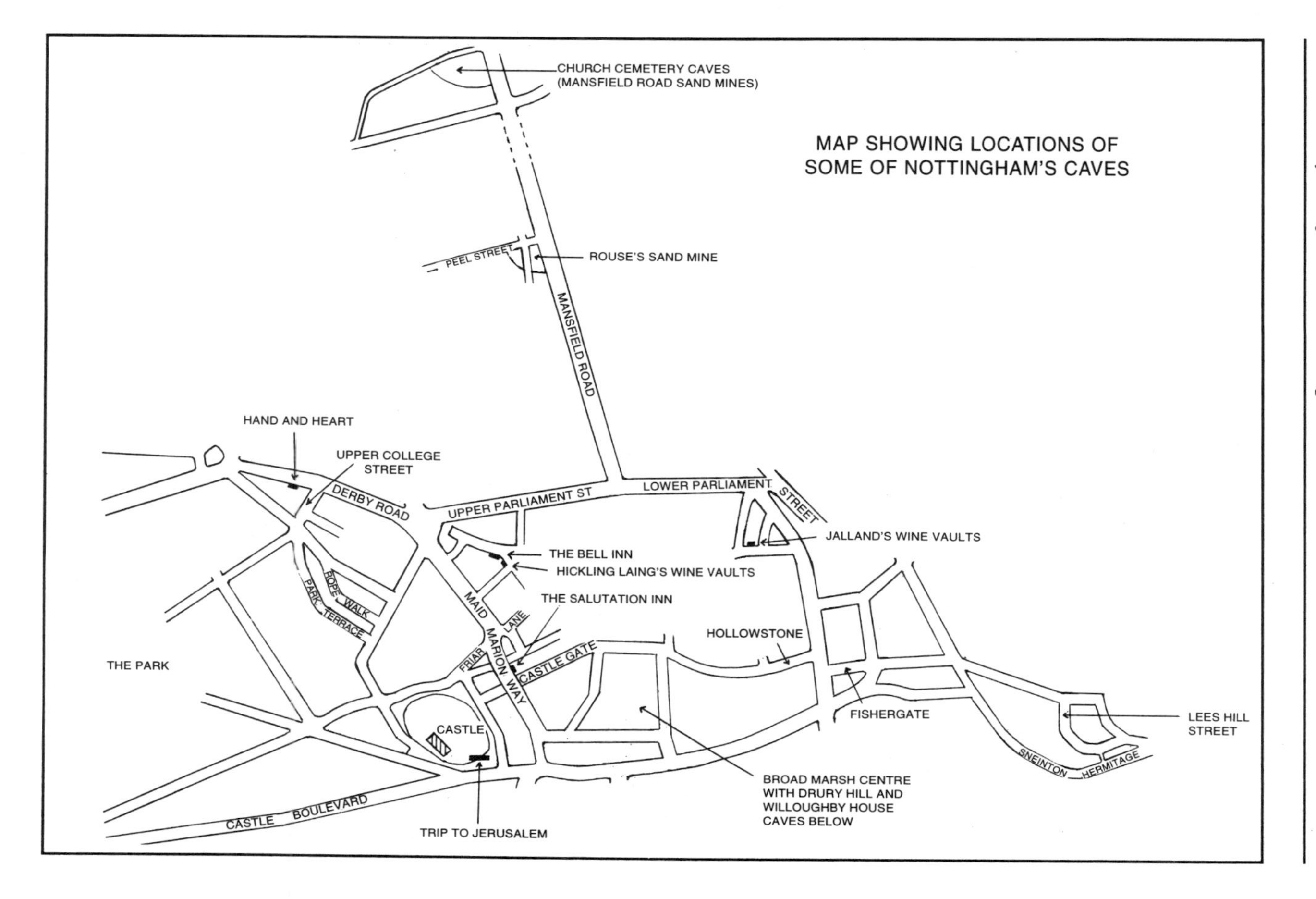
CHURCH CEMETERY CAVES (MANSFIELD ROAD SAND MINES)
MAP SHOWING LOCATIONS OF SOME OF NOTTINGHAM'S CAVES
PEEL STREET
ROUSE'S SAND MINE
MANSFIELD ROAD
HAND AND HEART
UPPER COLLEGE STREET
DERBY ROAD
UPPER PARLIAMENT ST
LOWER PARLIAMENT
STREET
JALLAND'S WINE VAULTS
THE BELL INN
HICKLING LAING'S WINE VAULTS
THE SALUTATION INN
HOLLOWSTONE
ROPE WALK
PARK TERRACE
MAID MARION WAY
LANE
FRIAR
CASTLE GATE
THE PARK
CASTLE
FISHERGATE
LEES HILL STREET
SNEINTON
HERMITAGE
BROAD MARSH CENTRE WITH DRURY HILL AND WILLOUGHBY HOUSE CAVES BELOW
CASTLE BOULEVARD
TRIP TO JERUSALEM

Row; in 1334, to excavations below the Daily Market at Weekday Cross, and in 1330, 1335 and 1336, to caves underneath Vout or Vault Lane, later Drury Hill. At one time a large house called Vouthalle or Vault Hall stood here, this, according to local historian Charles Deering '. . . had its name from very large vaults which were under it, where in the time of the Staple of Calais great quantities of wool used to be lodged. In one of these vaults, in the reign of King Charles II, the Dissenters privately met for the exercise of their religion.'

In the will of Richard Colier, 1368, we read of a 'store house for herrings situated opposite Nottingham Bridge', this probably being a reference to caves at Fishergate, and in 1407 there were complaints against one Richard Lee and others for 'throwing cinders and dung outside the wall of the township into the common caves blocking up the said caves.'

The number of excavations rapidly increased, a common type being the cesspit or garderobe of which hundreds existed. These had a round or square shaft opening out into a bell-shaped chamber and have often been found to contain artifacts dating virtually from the time of their construction. A fine medieval jug, the Knight Jug, now in the Castle Museum, was discovered in a cesspit below the Old Moot Hall in Friar Lane. Stone cut wells were also common; in medieval times most houses had their own well, these reaching down to the water table and, unlike wells in soft ground, not requiring any supporting masonry.

Tanning – the converting of animal skins to leather – was one of Nottingham's principal trades in medieval times and the Drury Hill Caves, preserved beneath the Broad Marsh Shopping Centre contained what may have been Britain's only subterranean tannery. This, the Tannery Cave, was about 33ft (10m) long, 16$^1/_2$ft (5m) wide and contained vats cut in the rock floor to hold the various solutions needed in the tanning process. It was in use by the 15th century and until 1639 was one of the many tanneries in this area, the smell from these being so appalling, it is said, that it even kept rats away and thus spared the district from the plague. Next to the Tannery Cave was an excavation known as the Pillar Cave, about the same size and containing a large central pillar and a cesspit in the floor, which yielded pottery dating from 1270 – 1300.

Dwelling caves existed at Sneinton Hermitage (described in more detail later) and in low cliffs along Mansfield Road, Derby Road and Hollow Stone. The corporation issued orders to evict the occupants of

Hollow Stone caves in 1606 '. . . they may be filled up and not made a harbour for beggars -Let it be done', yet vagrants were still living in the caves in 1975, when they were finally bricked-up. More elaborate was a group of caves known as Lenton Hermitage in the low cliff on the southern edge of the park. This included the Chapel of St Mary de La Roche and was the property of the Lenton Priory, founded In 1100. In a Pipe Roll document of 1244 it is recorded that King Henry III paid £6.ls.8d for the stipends of two Lenton monks ministering at the Chapel of St Mary in the Rock under the Castle. (*'In stipendus duorum monachorum ministrantium in Capella St Mariae de rupe subtus castrum de Notingham'*). It is not certain when the Rock Chapel ceased to be occupied but in 1524 it was reported that 'the lodgings in the Parke called "The Roche" is in dekay and ruyne in timber, lede, tile and glasse.' The rock dwellings were further damaged by Roundhead soldiers in 1651, those remaining are now hidden behind petrol stations on Castle Boulevard.

In subsequent years Nottingham's caves were used for a great variety of purposes, including the storage of wine and beer; hanging and salting meat; storing wool – as in the Drury Hill Caves; wagon making – carried on beneath Wollaton Street, and bank vaults. The caves under Peck Lane, destroyed in 1975, were used as bank vaults in Charles I's reign, by the same Mr Smith who founded Smith's Bank on the site. Many caves were adapted for use as air raid shelters during World War II, electric lights, roof-supports, buttresses and extra entrances being added. New purpose-built shelters were also excavated at Lees Hill, to the rear of Sneinton Hermitage, in Castle Rock and at several sites in the Radford district. The air-raid shelter under the Player's factory in Radford was reportedly able to shelter several thousand people. A council register for 1941 lists 77 caves available as public shelters.

'In World War II', a correspondent wrote to me, 'My sister trained as a nurse at Nottingham General Hospital and the network of caves/tunnels under that rocky outcrop were used for storing things like radium for the X-Ray machines. She went down there at times (during the '39-45 years) at night to collect radium needles for use in cancer treatment. Very eerie! There was one tunnel which was favoured by the doctors (and nurses), as the other end of it came out at the ancient pub 'The Trip to Jerusalem.'

I have been unable to find any further details of the tunnel between the hospital and the pub and despite old legends only a few relatively short passages are known today.

The Park Tunnel, looking towards The Park

The Park Tunnel, looking towards Derby Road

One of these, known as the Park Tunnel, was dug in 1856 under the direction of architect T.C. Hine to allow horse-drawn traffic to drive from Derby Road into the park; the first part was unlined and the second, beyond a huge well in the roof which admits light, was lined with brick. It is 246ft (75m) long, 26ft (8m) high and 26ft (8m) wide, large enough for two double-decker buses to pass one another. The tunnel was redundant even before its completion, other roads into the park having been built, but it survives as a pedestrian footpath.

Several passages were excavated within Castle Rock in medieval times, the earliest of which is thought to date from 1194. This linked the Castle with Brewhouse Yard at the base of the rock and was probably used to bring ale and other supplies into the castle. Another tunnel ran from the middle bailey of the castle towards the park in a westerly direction, much of this now being blocked. This tunnel is known as Davey Scot's Hole, perhaps having some connection with the old story (lacking historical foundation) that King David of Scotland, captured at the battle of Neville's Cross near Durham in 1346, was confined here for several years. A. Stapleton, in *Nottingham Caves* (1904) referred to another group of tunnels at Castle Rock:

'Another series of rock passages (one of them over 100yds in length) were laid open in 1899, on the westward extension of the castle plateau, when excavating for a new wing to the General Hospital. The spot is outside the medieval castle, but within the town defences. The north end of the main hospital building stands on the site of an ancient mound, on disturbing which, over a century ago, a dagger and several interments were found. Under this place a winding passage less than 4ft in height, and, consequently, only to be traversed in a stooping posture, led to a well over 100ft deep.'

All trace of these passages seems to have been lost. The Brewhouse Yard tunnel has for centuries been known as Mortimer's Hole, supposedly being the route by which the supporters of Edward III made their clandestine way into the castle in October 1330, to seize Roger Mortimer, Earl of March. Mortimer was the lover of Queen Isabel, mother of Edward, and the couple were thought by many to have usurped the power of the young king. Mortimer was taken to Westminster where he was tried and executed as a traitor, while Isabella was placed under house arrest at Castle Rising in Norfolk. However, some historians consider that another passage, perhaps Davey Scot's Hole, was the tunnel by which the King's supporters gained access to the castle.

Mortimer's Hole

Not surprisingly there are stories of ghosts in the area of Castle Rock: during World War II, for example, a group of American soldiers was walking past the Castle, close to the Trip to Jerusalem Inn, when they heard what seemed to be a woman's voice screaming in a foreign language. Was it Isabella shrieking in Norman French *'Bel fitz, eiez pitie du gentil Mortimer!'* – 'Fair son, have pity on sweet Mortimer!' as she is said to have done at the moment of her lover's capture?

Most of Nottingham's caves are not open to the public, but there are regular tours of Mortimer's Hole (a notice in the Castle warns that these are not suitable for infirm people – much of the city centre is hilly) and it is possible to visit a cave used as an air raid shelter which is now part of the Brewhouse Yard museum. Volunteer groups occasionally organise tours to the caves of Drury Hill, Shire Hall and Bridlesmith Gate and some pub cellar caves can be seen by appointment. The Park Tunnel is also accessible, perhaps most easily approached via the steps which lead down from a metal gateway in Upper College Street and the few remaining caves of Sneinton Hermitage can be seen from the road. Some of the city's caves are described in more detail in the following pages.

Beer Cellars and Wine Vaults

Many of the city's excavations are associated with the making and storage of ale. Malting – the transforming of barley into malt – was one of Nottingham's principal trades from the 13th century onwards, the process being carried out in subterranean kilns, hewn out of the solid rock. Typically, a kiln would be a circular room up to 13ft (4m) across, with a ledge around a central pit. There would be an entrance hole at the bottom of the pit, allowing the stoking of a fire, and another entrance higher up, giving access to the grain which was roasted on a grill resting on the circular ledge. There were usually adjacent caves, one used for storage, perhaps, another containing a well and one in which the grain was allowed to germinate, converting its starch to sugar, before it was roasted. Eighteen malt-kiln caves have been discovered in Nottingham, good examples being those underneath Drury Hill, now covered by the Broad Marsh Shopping Centre, and Castle Gate. All the kiln caves have been damaged by later building above, the most intact being that at Castle Gate which is unusual in that a rock-cut privy or garderobe is also present, disconcertingly close to the well. The garderobe was found to contain sherds of pottery dating from about 1250.

Many of Nottingham's inns and taverns brewed their own ale, having bought the malt from the kiln owners, the constant temperature below ground being ideal for both brewing and the storage of the finished product. From the earliest days, Nottingham was noted for the quality of its beer. Celia Fiennes, after visiting the city in the late-17th century, wrote:

'Nottingham is famous for good ale so for cellars. They are all dug out of the rocks and so are very coole, att the Crown Inn is a cellar of 60 stepps down all in the Rock like arch worke over your head, in the Cellar I drank good ale.'

Most of these pub cellars are about 20ft to 26ft (6 – 8m) long by 10ft to 13ft (3 – 4m) wide and have one rounded end. Generally, the rock roof above is about 6$^{1}/_{2}$ft (2m) thick, but deeper cellars are known, those beneath the Lion Hotel in Clumber Street, for example, having about 16ft (5m) of rock above them, the cellar floor being just above the water table. The cellar caves have low ledges cut out of their walls, these being known as thralls and which supported the barrels, allowing ale to be drawn off easily. Thralls often had to be repaired or rebuilt with brick after years of use had worn away the stone. The rock roofs of the cellars often had holes cut through to allow barrels to be hoisted in and out. The Crown Inn where Celia Fiennes drank, and its cellars, have since long gone, but other public houses still possess their ancient cellars, the most extensive of these being beneath the Salutation Inn on Maid Marion Way. The cellars here are large enough to have been used for brewing as well as storing ale and the earliest sections may date, like the pub itself, from the 15th century. Rock cut cellars can also be seen at the Bell Inn, the Hand and Heart and Ye Olde Trip to Jerusalem. In the latter, customers can drink in a bar entirely within a cave.

Cellars at Ye Olde Trip to Jerusalem

In the mid-19th century the Nottingham Brewery dug extensive cellars beneath its site on Mansfield Road, these now being underneath York House. These excavations broke through into earlier caves beneath the Yorker Inn, and a later extension to the Brewery's cellars was a tunnel which opened out into Victoria Station and allowed the beer barrels to be taken directly from the brewery to railway wagons. The exit is now sealed behind a retaining wall built later in the railway cutting. Huge cellars were also excavated between 1852 and 1880 beneath Shipstone's Brewery on Radford Road, in the Basford district, these consisting of nine panelled rooms each 55yds (50m) long and 16ft (5m) wide.

Wine was also stored underground, as at the Hickling Liang wine vaults beneath Gascoines, the estate agents, in Angel Row. The vaults which contain brick wine racks are about 200 years old and are reached by rock steps which cut through older cellars used as storage rooms, above them. A large shaft also descends to the vaults, at the bottom of which are rails on which stood barrels. Other wine cellars included Jalland's Vaults, beneath Goose Gate, and Skinner and Rook's vaults underneath the Guildhall. The latter were cut in about 1860 and adopted for use as the local Civil Defence headquarters in World War II, after being extensively reinforced.

The largest of the three rooms comprising the Willoughby Wine Cellars

In 1738 the Honourable Rothwell Willoughby built a house on Low Pavement, Drury Hill, beneath which he excavated a wine cellar consisting of three circular rooms, each of which has a central pillar with a circular rock table. The largest cave is about 25ft (7.5m) across and has a perimeter thrall. The two smaller caves have brick wine bins. Charles

Deering, the local historian, visited the cellars shortly after their completion, commenting in his book *The History of Nottinghamshire* (1751):

'The passage leading down to them opens to the North, is arched and has 32 easy Steps, cover'd with Bricks, and receives light enough to make the descent pleasant. At the bottom you meet with three Doors: that which faces you leads to the greatest Cellar; the other two on each side give entrance into two lesser Cellars. All three describe circles, having hemispherical Roofs. The Centre of each is supported by a proportionable round Pillar of Rock. The lesser have Bings [ledges or thralls] all round them; and what is peculiarly remarkable is, that in so large an extent of Rock, requisite for such considerable Excavations, there does not appear the least Crack or Flaw.'

Sand Mines

The Nottingham Castle Sandstone is very friable and has been mined extensively for sand. This was used both in building and, in former times, for spreading on the floors of houses and public buildings, to absorb dirt. Some sand was mined at the surface but the best deposits were underground and these could be excavated without the problem of land ownership that surface working entailed. Two sand mines existed in the Mansfield Road area of Nottingham, the largest of these being Rouse's Mine which extended underground between Mansfield Road and Peel Street. (The land above, Sand Field, was common land where mining would have been prohibited). According to John Blackner, in the introduction to his *History of Nottingham* (1815):

'This cave, which is the largest in the town, is the work of one James Ross, or Rouse, who, during thirty years, got sand in it, which he sold to the good housewives of the town to scatter upon their floors. Old age and infirmities compelled him a few years ago, to cease from his labour and he retired to spend the remainder of his days in St Nicholas's Workhouse.'

Rouse's mine was a haphazard, hand-worked, pillar-and-stall excavation, the stalls, or worked areas, generally being between 6$^1/_2$ and 10ft (2 – 3m) across, while some of the larger 'rooms' were about 16ft (5m) wide. The workings followed the horizontal beds of sandstone, there being two levels each of about 6$^1/_2$ft (2m) high. These are mainly connected with each other but in places are quite separate, the upper level being divided from the lower by a rock floor. Access, from

Mansfield Road, was by the drift method, rather than by shafts, and donkeys may have been used to haul the sand underground. There were almost certainly older caves on the site prior to Rouse's activities and parts of these may now form part of the underground galleries to the north of the mine's entrance off Mansfield Road. Paupers once lived in caves alongside Mansfield Road and town records of 1335 and 1595 refer to 'todeholes', these perhaps being caves occupied by lepers.

It is thought that Rouse's mine yielded some ten thousand tons of sand before working ceased with his retirement to St Nicholas's workhouse in the late-18th century. Subsequently, its existence seems to have been forgotten until 1837 when, according to A. Stapleton writing in 1904, a man become lost in it for five hours after he rediscovered the mine. Stapleton continues:

'Still more unfortunate were two other men who, the day following, attempted an exploration. Having first lost their bearings, they were subsequently set upon by a gang of ruffians. One managed to hide himself in a recess, but the other was robbed and severely beaten. Many years ago the late Andrew MacCullum, a well-known painter, produced a curious effect at the extremity of this excavation by the judicious use of whitewash and lamp-black, notably a representation of a recumbent figure on a tomb.'

When the new houses were built along Mansfield Road in the mid-19th century their foundations were cut through the mine to reach solid rock beneath, probably destroying original entrance holes. In 1892, the mine became a tourist attraction, being advertised, absurdly, as Robin Hood's Mammoth Cave, and during World War II it was used as an air-raid shelter, two new entrances with steps being cut through the rock at the north end of the mine. One of these, on Peel Street, is now the only way into the mine.

Further north there were more sand mines around Gallows Hill, these being associated with sand quarries which in the 18th century lay on both sides of Mansfield Road. This was waste land where people dug their own sand. There were originally three quarries in a line working southward into the slope of the Mount Hooten escarpment and two of these eventually went underground, becoming drift entered, pillar-and-stall, workings, similar to Rouse's mine but not so large. Parts of one of the old mines, known as the Mine Caves, still exist to the east of Mansfield Road, behind the old quarry wall. To the west of the road, on the site now occupied by Rock Cemetery, there was a similar quarry and mine. The latter seems to have been a well-organised enterprise as it had an underground, horse-drawn, narrow-gauge railway. However, it seems that insufficient rock was left supporting the roof, part of which collapsed in 1806, killing a man. In 1811, more of the roof was broken down on the orders of the corporation, as a safety measure. The Cemetery Caves, which comprised part of the workings, and the remains of the pillars from the collapsed section can still be seen at the Rock Cemetery.

The third quarry had no mine and was landscaped into a circular amphitheatre, this probably being undertaken between 1859 and 1863 when the Catacomb Caves were excavated from a tunnel linking this quarry with the adjacent one (see plan). It was intended that the Catacomb Caves should be an underground burial place, but the project foundered when the contractor went bankrupt. The Mine Caves, to the east of Mansfield Road, were, like Rouse's caves, adapted to form an air-raid shelter during World War II, an entrance being provided off Mansfield Road, and two short tunnels were dug to link its three sections together.

A gallery in Rouse's Sand Mine

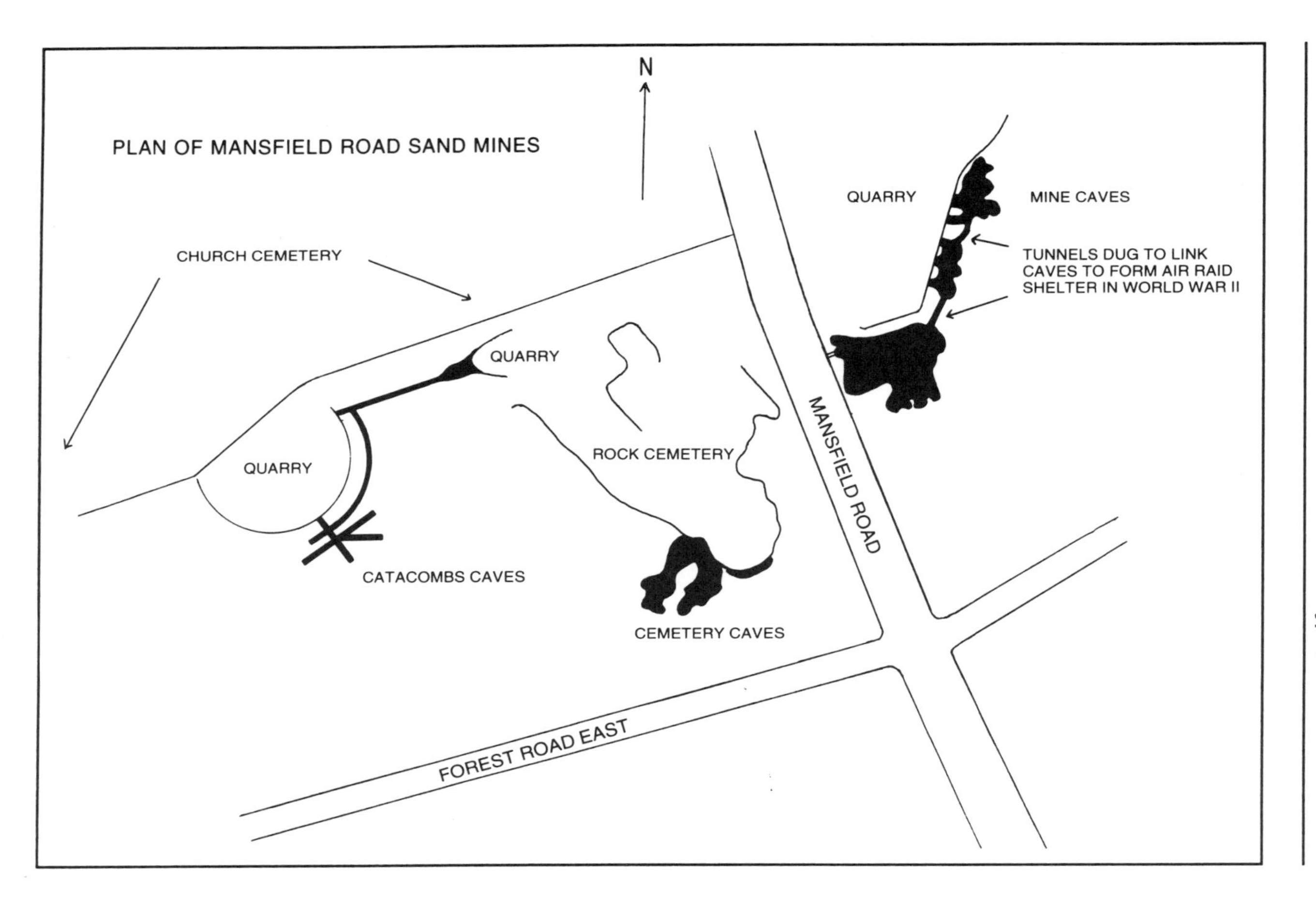
PLAN OF MANSFIELD ROAD SAND MINES
N
CHURCH CEMETERY
QUARRY
MINE CAVES
TUNNELS DUG TO LINK CAVES TO FORM AIR RAID SHELTER IN WORLD WAR II
QUARRY
QUARRY
ROCK CEMETERY
MANSFIELD ROAD
CATACOMBS CAVES
CEMETERY CAVES
FOREST ROAD EAST

Sneinton Hermitage

The largest collection of subterranean dwellings in Nottingham was known as Sneinton Hermitage, lying to the east of the town centre, where cave dwellings were excavated in the entire length of a sandstone bluff some 328yds (295m) long. The earliest written reference to the hermitage appears to be in a rental document dating from 1544, which reads: 'Item, there is a house under the ground in a roche of stone that sometyme was called thermitage.' A later rental of 1591 refers to 'The Ermytage in Sneynton being a house cutte oute of rock, and paieth yearly 2s.' These entries refer to a specific cave, or group of caves, which was occupied by a medieval hermit, the name hermitage later being applied to the whole line of the cliff. Which of the caves was the original hermitage has never been established, but it could have been a large cavern which was destroyed during building work in 1903 and which is described in more detail below. As time went by, walls and house fronts were added to the caves, and finally whole buildings, such as public houses, were built in front of some of them, the caves then being used as store-rooms. *Laird's Beauties of England and Wales* (1814) described the hermitage as follows:

'Great part of the village, indeed, consists of the habitations within the rock, many of which have staircases that lead up to gardens on the top, and some of them hanging on shelves on its sides. To a stranger it is extremely curious to see the perpendicular face of the rock with its doors and windows in tiers, and the inhabitants peeping out from their dens like the inmates of another world: in fact, if it were *not at home*, and therefore *of no value*, it would, without doubt, have been novelized and melodramatised, until all the fashionable world had been mad for getting under ground. The coffee-house and ale-houses, cut out of the rock, are the common resort of the holiday folks: indeed the coffee-house is not only extremely pleasant from its garden plats, and arbours in front, but also extremely curious from its great extent into the body of the rock, where visitors may almost choose their degree of temperature on the hottest day of summer.'

The cave dwellings were each about 10ft (3m) across and 30ft (9m) deep with cupboards and shelves cut into the rock. Some were white-washed and, where one room opened into another, carefully situated openings allowed daylight into inner chambers. Others were larger, there being, for example, a rock-cut dance-hall behind the Earl Manvers

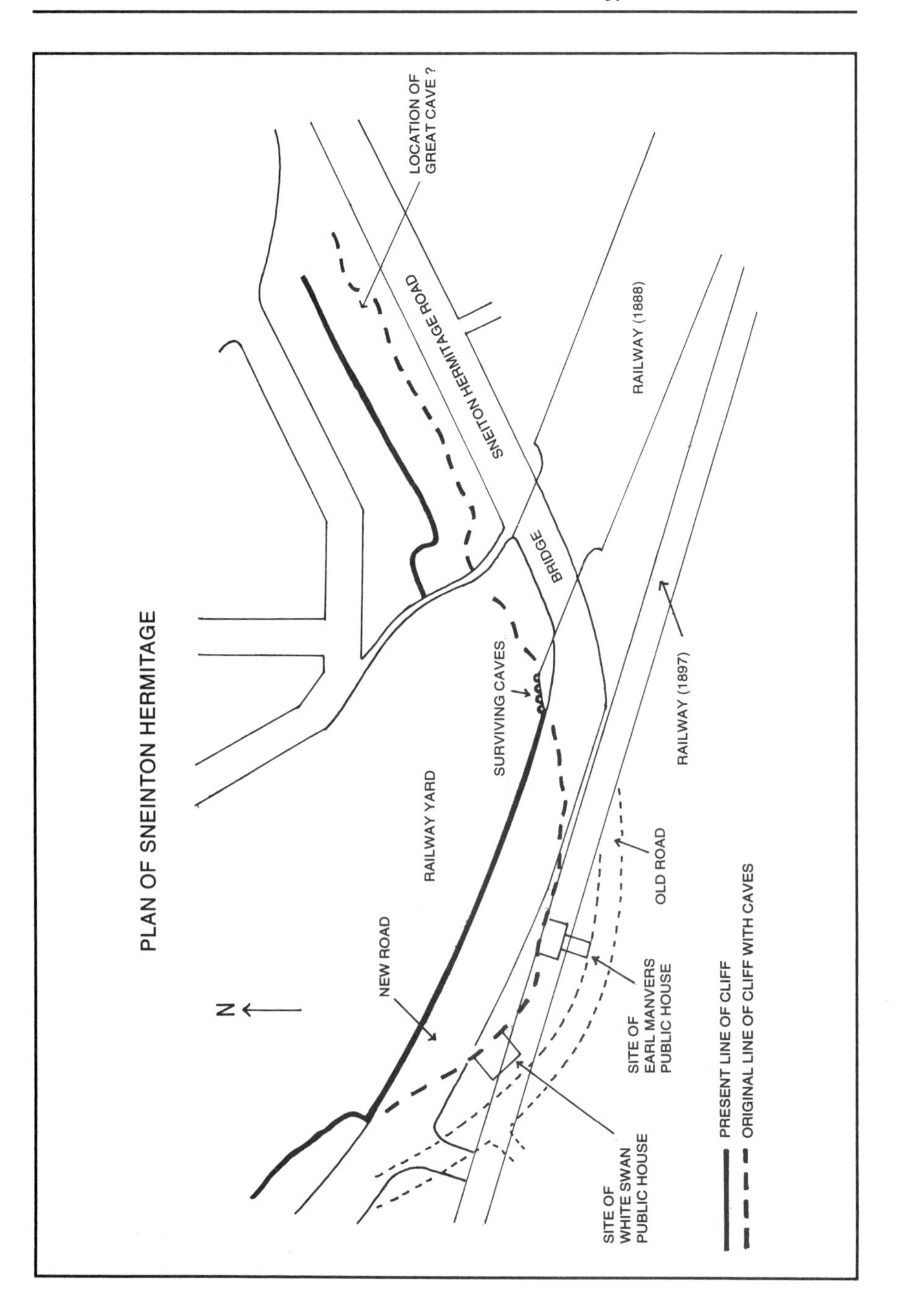
PLAN OF SNEINTON HERMITAGE
N
LOCATION OF GREAT CAVE ?
SNEITON HERMITAGE ROAD
RAILWAY (1888)
BRIDGE
SURVIVING CAVES
RAILWAY YARD
RAILWAY (1897)
OLD ROAD
NEW ROAD
SITE OF EARL MANVERS PUBLIC HOUSE
SITE OF WHITE SWAN PUBLIC HOUSE
PRESENT LINE OF CLIFF
ORIGINAL LINE OF CLIFF WITH CAVES

public house on the western edge of the hermitage. Some caverns had their own wells, one press account from the 1890s reporting:

'In two or three of the rock houses there is a well, or cistern, cut out of the rock at the bottom of a flight of steps, the permanent water level being only about 10ft or 12ft below the level of the road here. Thus the cottagers were able to provide their own water supply without going out of doors for it.'

The report also mentions that one of the caves had evidently been used as a stable, since a manger had been hewn out of the rock. There is a record of a visit to the eastern caves at about the same time by a group of local dignitaries which included Alderman Fredrick Pullman, Mr J. Potter, the borough librarian and Mr Blasdale the local agent of Lord Manvers on whose land the hermitage was situated. The party was conducted by Mr W.R. James of Sneinton Hollows, the entrance to one of the caves being in his back garden. One cave was used for growing mushrooms and storing turnips, the excavation containing a well. Another was used as a dairy, while a third was used for storing beer barrels. The most impressive cavern was that described later by a local historian A. Stapleton in *Bygone Nottingham* (1903) and *Nottingham Caves* (1904):

'To the rear of one house are two small open excavations, hewn at right angles with a narrow passage leading to a long flight of steps which bring one into an extensive chamber supported by seven square pillars, 12 feet in circumference, from 18 to 20ft in height. The cave is divided into a number of apartments, two of which are at a higher elevation than the rest; the floor of these at the far end, which are lighted by rough windows hewn out of the rock at the entrance, is over 10ft below the level of the passage. The chimney appears to have been situated to the left near the entrance where it pierced the rocky roof.'

This, Stapleton believed, might have been the original hermitage cave. It seems that some caves were still used as habitations as late as the 1860s. Most of them were destroyed about the turn of the century when the cliff face was cut back. This occurred in three stages, the first being in 1888, when the central section of the bluff was removed to allow a branch line of the London and North Western Railway to reach into a yard built on a terrace cut into Lees Hill behind the hermitage. Then, in 1896, the western caves were destroyed when the cliff was cut back during construction of the Great Northern line which led into Nottingham Victoria station. Finally, in 1903, the eastern caves were lost, when the road, named Sneinton Hermitage, was widened and new houses were built on its north side. A small group of caves did survive, however, and these can still be seen in the Sneinton Hermitage road, at the site of the now demolished 1888 railway bridge.

The Earl Manvers Public House

In 1903 the *Nottingham Weekly Express* sent a reporter to interview a Miss Eleanor Boulderson who was born In Sneinton in 1819, and who had clear memories of the hermitage and its inhabitants. Her recollections appeared in the 24th April edition of the paper under the heading 'Sneinton of the past. An interview with the oldest villager.' One hermitage family, Miss Boulderson recalled, by the name of Tansley, kept their horse in their rock house – which supports the 1890s report of a manger in one of the caves -while another of the caves was occupied by a man named Beecroft (suspected locally of being a Luddite) who made a living by excavating sand in his cave and selling it to housewives for spreading on the floors. It was popularly believed that he had tunnelled as far as Sneinton Church before being forbidden by the authorities to burrow any further for fear that the church might collapse. It was also believed that, in one of Beecroft's tunnels, a madman was kept chained to the wall. One of Miss Boulderson's most vivid memories was that of the Sneinton rock fall of 1829, which became part of local folklore and which was caused, apparently, by the hermitage dwellers tunnelling ever deeper into the hillside, leaving hundreds of tons of rock almost unsupported. She recalled:

'It occurred about midnight. It was the day before Barton Wake, and the sons of Mrs Flinders, who lived in one of the houses, had arranged to take their mother to the wake by boat. That night the sons were alarmed by the barking of their little dog, and on going into the cave to see what was the matter they saw that the rocks had split in twain. They rushed to their mother, pulled her out of bed, and carried her out as the whole thing collapsed.'

The White Swan public house

Contemporary press accounts confirm Miss Boulderson's detail of the barking of the dog and provide additional information. At about 2 o'clock on the morning of Sunday, 10th May, the landlord of the White

Swan, Mr Eyre, was awakened by a huge mass of earth and rock falling through the roof of the back premises of the building, into the room next to that in which he was sleeping. Mr Eyre hurried next door to warn the Flinders family, who, as Miss Boulderson recalled, had already been awakened by their dog. The two families – the Flinders and the Eyres – hastily vacated their houses and in the road outside were joined by several neighbours. The *Nottingham and Newark Mercury* continues:

'At four o'clock the expected event took place; a cracking noise was heard, and the whole face of the rock fell in huge masses and totally buried the house of Mr Flinders, so as to entirely obscure it from sight: whilst the habitable part of Mr Eyre's was also much beaten in. The spectators of this catastrophe had only sufficient time to run with all their speed to escape the tumbling masses . . . '

Following the rock fall, work was undertaken to remove further sections of the cliff which overhung the houses, and while this was in progress a second fall occurred, a gigantic piece of rock, weighing several tons, crashing down on to the rear premises of the Manvers Arms public house. The landlady, Mrs Seymour, was showered with debris but escaped injury; even luckier was a workman standing on the rock when it fell, who leapt to safety just in time.

Sneinton Hermitage, showing house-fronts built onto caves

The remaining Sneinton Hermitage caves

An Alderman's Folly

The excavations discussed so far have all had a practical purpose but the caves of Alderman Thomas Herbert, a wealthy 19th century lace manufacturer, were an architectural folly, created to add interest to the gardens of his house on The Ropewalk, overlooking the park. (Many years ago rope was made in this area, hemp being grown locally). The gardens sloped downwards into the Park Valley and each main cave had a staircase entry at the rear and opened out horizontally onto the terrace below. The caves were excavated over a number of years and their layout can be followed by reference to the simplified plan.

At the highest level is the Columns Cave, a rectangular chamber with a roof supported by eighteen square stone pillars in three rows of six. The columns are each about 8ft (2.5m) high. In the north wall of the cave are several niches, each containing a statue, though the figures are now very worn, while in the south Wall is a recess containing a crucifix. The Columns Cave was originally connected to another cave at the rear but this has been filled in to support the land above, now a car park.

In front of the Columns Cave, further down the garden slope, is a cave known as The Herbarium or Greenhouse, this apparently having been used by the girls of a nearby school in Victorian times. This excavation is two caves, linked by a passageway, each containing a stone trough about 3ft (1m) high, in which plants were grown. The trough in the far cave had a hollow base, next to which a fireplace had been built so that hot air would circulate beneath the plants. This cave was well-lit by a large window overlooking the park and originally glazed with coloured glass.

In the most impressive of the caves is a sculpture depicting Daniel in the Lions' Den, carved out of the rear wall, the whole scene being about 10ft (3m) high and 13ft (4m) wide. The stone figures have suffered from weathering and vandalism over the years, one end of the cave being open to the elements and for a long period unprotected. Daniel and one of the six lions have lost their heads – Daniel has also lost an arm and some of the lions' limbs are missing. This cave also contains four columns round a ribbed dome in the roof which is topped by a skylight, while in the wall opposite the tableau are a door and two windows, originally of stained glass. A date, 1856, was at one time visible in the wall of the cave but being close to one of the windows has completely weathered away. A doorway in the north-west wall of this cave opens

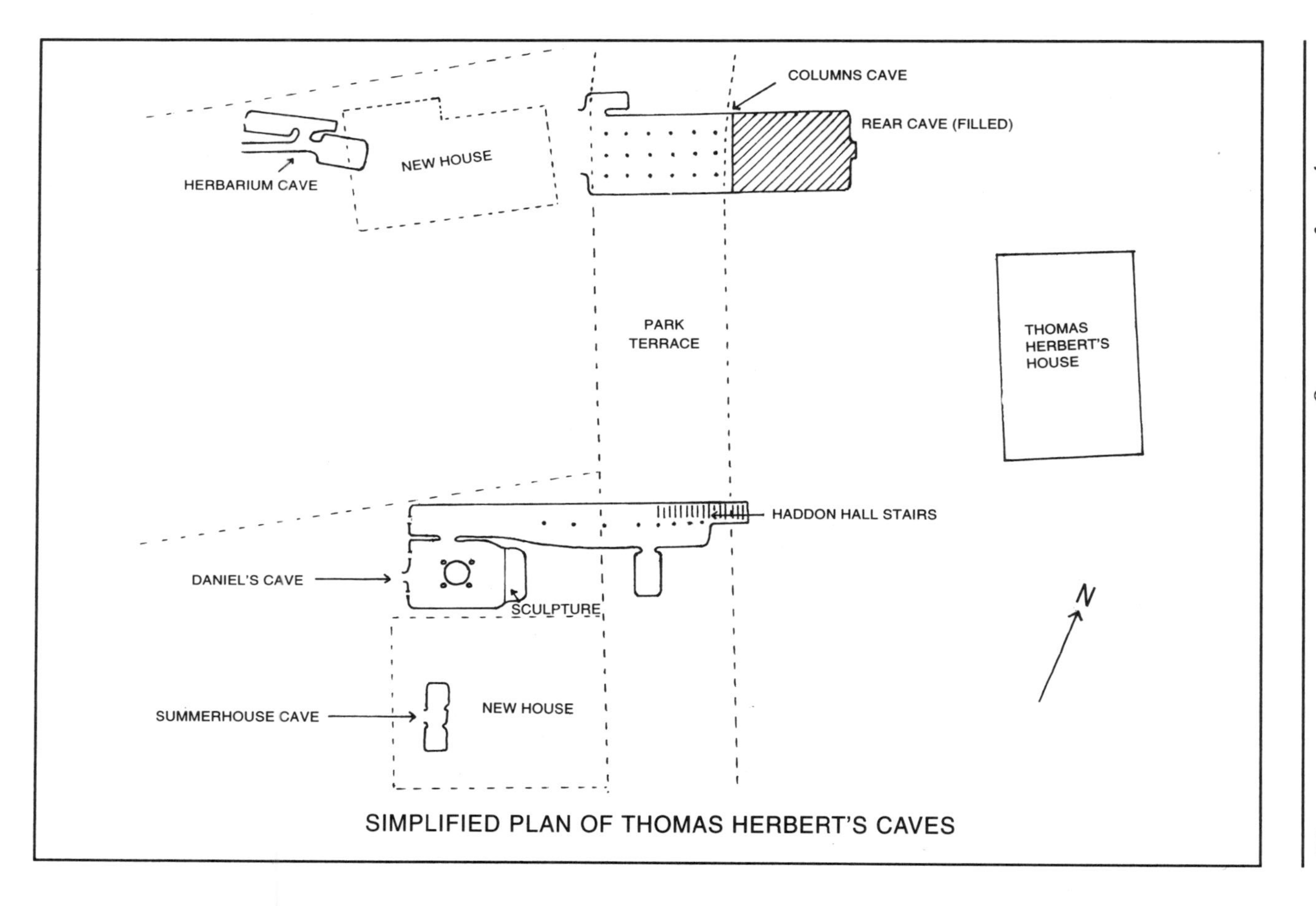

SIMPLIFIED PLAN OF THOMAS HERBERT'S CAVES

into a wide passageway; on the wall immediately opposite is carved a shield bearing the initials of Thomas Herbert, and to the left the passage terminates with another window, formerly of stained glass.

Daniel's cave

In this passage are niches containing stone figures (one of which is almost completely worn away) said to represent Druidical figures – a Chief Priest and a Sacrificial Priest. There is also a recess containing a sculpted pillar, much worn, around which climbs a vine, or possibly a snake. Sloping upwards to the right, the passage contains eight stone pillars, near the fourth of which is an entry to a side cave, with a domed roof and a trough encircling the walls, the purpose of which is unclear.

Back again in the passage, by the 5th pillar a staircase about 14ft (4.25m) long, with a balustrade carved into the left-hand wall, leads up to a landing, from which another flight, also 14ft (4.25m) long continues up to the surface and a doorway, now bricked up, on the far side of which is the car park. (This staircase, which passes beneath Park Terrace, is said to be a copy of one in Haddon Hall). The total length of the passage, from the bricked-up doorway to the far window, is 90ft (27m) and the bottom of the lower staircase is 32ft (9.5m) below the level of the blocked up entrance. In the wall of the south-west side of the landing is carved the figure of a seated man playing a harp, which appears to represent a Druidical bard.

Adjacent to Daniel's Cave and on the same terrace, is the Summer-house or Grotto, in the walls of which are carved a variety of animal forms, including snakes, birds, monkeys, crocodiles and bats. In recesses in the walls are set ornamental blocks of a volcanic stone known as tufa, thought to have been brought from the Lake District. On either side of the doorway at the front of the cave are window openings, above one of which are carved, again, Alderman Herbert's initials and the date 1872. The latter, compared with the date 1856 in Daniel's Cave, gives an indication of the time-span over which the caves were constructed.

Sadly, these remarkable caves are no longer accessible to the public, as they are now incorporated in the gardens of new houses along Park Terrace. Perhaps at some time they may be restored and opened to visitors.

The Burrowing Duke

England has a long tradition of eccentric aristocrats, one of the strangest being the 5th Duke of Portland, William John Cavendish Bentinck-Scott, born in 1800, whose passion for solitude was so extreme it led to rumours that he was hideously diseased or disfigured (in fact, he was a handsome man). Perhaps it was his dislike of being seen that led to his obsession with excavating tunnels and underground rooms at the family estate of Welbeck Abbey in north Nottinghamshire, his contemporaries often referring to him as 'the burrowing duke.' One description of the Duke's excavations is given by the diarist Augustus Hare in his autobiography *In My Solitary Life* (abridged edition, 1953), Hare having visited Welbeck in 1882, three years after the Duke's death:

'The Duke's mania for a hidden life made him build immense suites of rooms underground, only approachable by a common flight of steps leading to a long tunnel, down which the dinner is conveyed from the far-distant kitchen on a tramway. From a great library one enters a billiard-room capable of holding half-a-dozen billiard-tables. A third large room leads to an enormous ball-room which can contain 2000 people. The approach to this from above is by means of a gigantic hydraulic drop, in which a carriage can be placed, or twenty persons can be accommodated – the guests being thus let down to the ball-room itself. A staircase through the ceiling of one of the rooms, which is drawn up by a windlass, leads hence to the old riding-school, which is lighted by 1000 jets of gas. Hence, a tunnel, 200yds long, leads to a quadrangle piece of ground unbuilt upon, but excavated in preparation for a large range of bachelor's rooms, smoking-rooms, and nurseries to cover four acres of ground. Another tunnel, three quarters of a mile long, leads thence to the stables, cow-houses, and dairies.'

The 5th Duke died at Harcourt House, his London home, in December 1879, the Dukedom passing to his first-cousin-once-removed who immediately travelled to Welbeck with his step-mother, stepbrothers and sister, the family moving into the four or five rooms that the late Duke had occupied. The day after their arrival they began to explore the huge house and the underground passages. The 6th Duke's sister, Lady Ottoline Morrell, later recalled coming across:

'...three underground rooms, all very large, and one that seemed quite immense. These were painted pink with parquet floors, heated by hot air, and lit from the top by mushroom lights – level with the ground so that in the daytime they were quite light and at night were lit by gas chandeliers. There was no beauty in them – they were just vast empty rooms, built down instead of up, and except for the top lighting you would not have been aware that they were under the level of the ground. Along the side of them was a glass corridor intended for statues, but with no statues.

'Then back we came to the house through more underground passages. Starting from these passages was the walking tunnel, about a mile long and wide enough for two or three people to walk abreast, that led from the house to the stables and gardens; and a little way off and parallel to it was another, rather rougher one, for the use of the gardeners and workmen; for the Duke did not wish to meet anyone walking in the same tunnel as himself. Then there was the great driving tunnel, more than a mile long, which was the only direct road to Worksop. It had been dug out under the old drive and was wide enough for two carriages to pass each other. In the daytime it was lit from the top by small mushroom windows which threw a ghostly light upon it, except where it dipped down under the lake, and there it was lit by jets of gas, as was the whole tunnel at night.'

Northern entrance to the 5th Duke of Portland's driving tunnel

The brick-lined driving tunnel is 1$^{1}/_{4}$ml (2km) long and reached from the Duke's stables at Holbeck almost to the edge of Worksop, passing under the lake and the Abbey itself. The Duke would begin his journeys to London at the stables, his carriage, with green silk blinds, being driven through the tunnel and thence to Worksop Station. At the station the carriage was lifted, with the Duke inside, on to a flat railway wagon and conveyed to London where it was driven through the streets, still with drawn blinds, to Harcourt House.

Welbeck Abbey is now a college owned by the Ministry of Defence, the family occupying a house about a mile away built by the 7th Duke in the early 1930s and the 5th Duke's subterranean follies are inaccessible to the public. However, it is possible to see some surface evidence of his activities. Travelling north along the main A60 road one passes the B6042 Creswell road on the left and about a mile (1.5km) further on a long unsignposted track called Broad Lane turns off to the right. This quiet lane eventually leads to a building which resembles the castellated entrance to a railway tunnel, flanked by twin lodges. This is the northern entrance to the Duke's driving tunnel.

Despite his eccentricities, the 5th Duke of Portland seems to have been a kindly man. Lady Ottoline described how he provided the hundreds of labourers who carried out his excavations with donkeys to carry them to and from their work and large silk umbrellas to shelter them from the rain. His servants and tenants were devoted to him, his generous donations to charity well-known, and it is possible that one purpose of his excavations was to employ poor people during hard times. Certainly, his successors were noted for their philanthropic works but in more conventional ways.

Index

We publish a wide range of titles, including general interest publications, guides to individual towns, and books for outdoor activities centred on walking and cycling in the great outdoors throughout England and Wales. This is a recent selection:

General interest:

THE INCREDIBLY BIASED BEER GUIDE – Ruth Herman
This is the most comprehensive guide to Britain's smaller breweries and the pubs where you can sample their products. Produced with the collaboration of the Small Independent Brewers' Association and including a half-price subscription to The Beer Lovers' Club. *£6.95*

DIAL 999 – EMERGENCY SERVICES IN ACTION – John Creighton
Re-live the excitement as fire engines rush to disasters. See dramatic rescues on land and sea. Read how the professionals keep a clear head and swing into action. *£9.95*

THE ALABAMA AFFAIR – David Hollett
This is an account of Britain's rôle in the American Civil War. Read how Merseyside dockyards supplied ships for the Confederate navy, thereby supporting the slave trade. The *Alabama* was the most famous of the 'Laird Rams', and was chased half way across the world before being sunk ignominiously. *£9.95*

PEAK DISTRICT DIARY – Roger Redfern
An evocative book, celebrating the glorious countryside of the Peak District. The book is based on Roger's popular column in *The Guardian* newspaper and is profusely illustrated with stunning photographs. *£6.95*

I REMAIN, YOUR SON JACK – J. C. Morten (edited by Sheila Morten)
A collection of almost 200 letters, as featured on BBC TV, telling the moving story of a young soldier in the First World War. Profusely illustrated with contemporary photographs. *£8.95*

FORGOTTEN DIVISIONS – John Fox
A unique account of the 1914 – 18 War, drawing on the experience of soldiers and civilians, from a Lancashire town and a Rhineland village. The book is well illustrated and contains many unique photographs. *£9.95*

ROAD SENSE – Doug Holland
A book for drivers with some experience, preparing them for an advanced driving test. The book introduces a recommended system of car control, based on that developed by the Police Driving School. Doug Holland is a highly qualified driving instructor, working with RoSPA. *£5.95*

Books of Walks:

There are many books for outdoor people in our catalogue, including:

RAMBLES IN NORTH WALES
– Roger Redfern

HERITAGE WALKS IN THE PEAK DISTRICT
– Clive Price

EAST CHESHIRE WALKS
– Graham Beech

WEST CHESHIRE WALKS
– Jen Darling

WEST PENNINE WALKS
– Mike Cresswell

STAFFORDSHIRE WALKS
– Les Lumsdon

NEWARK AND SHERWOOD RAMBLES
– Malcolm McKenzie

NORTH NOTTINGHAMSHIRE RAMBLES
– MAlcolm McKenzie

RAMBLES AROUND NOTTINGHAM & DERBY
– Keith Taylor

RAMBLES AROUND MANCHESTER
– Mike Cresswell

WESTERN LAKELAND RAMBLES
– Gordon Brown

WELSH WALKS:
Dolgellau and the Cambrian Coast
– Laurence Main and Morag Perrott

WELSH WALKS:
Aberystwyth and District
– Laurence Main and Morag Perrott

MOSTLY DOWNHILL:
Leisurely walks in the Lake District
– Alan Pears

WEST PENNINE WALKS
– Mike Cresswell

– all of the above books are currently £6.95 each

CHALLENGING WALKS IN NORTH-WEST BRITAIN
– Ron Astley *(£9.95)*

WALKING PEAKLAND TRACKWAYS
– Mike Cresswell *(£7.95)*

Long-distance walks:

For long-distance walks enthusiasts, we have several books including:

THE GREATER MANCHESTER BOUNDARY WALK
– Graham Phythian

THE THIRLMERE WAY
– Tim Cappelli

THE FURNESS TRAIL
– Tim Cappelli

THE MARCHES WAY
– Les Lumsdon

THE TWO ROSES WAY
– Peter Billington, Eric Slater,
Bill Greenwood and Clive Edwards

THE RED ROSE WALK
– Tom Schofield

FROM WHARFEDALE TO WESTMORLAND:
Historical walks through the Yorkshire Dales
– Aline Watson

THE WEST YORKSHIRE WAY
– Nicholas Parrott

– all £6.95 each

The Best Pub Walks!

Sigma publish the widest range of "Pub Walks" guides, covering just about every popular walking destination in England and Wales. Each book includes 25 – 30 interesting walks and varied suitable for individuals or family groups. *The walks are based on "Real Ale" inns of character and are all accessible by public transport.*

Areas covered include

Cheshire • Dartmoor • Exmoor • Isle of Wight • Yorkshire Dales • Peak District • Lake District • Cotswolds • Mendips • Cornwall • Lancashire • Oxfordshire • Snowdonia • Devon

... and dozens more – all £6.95 each!